2020 DECISION:

SOCIALISM, RACISM OR HAPPINESS?

(An outsider's perspective.)

Joan Williams BSc, is a Jamaican who was educated in Canada, USA and Jamaica. Her initial training was in computer programming but she decided very early that she preferred to work with humans *not* machines. She then got involved in Public Relations and politics in Jamaica before moving on to become a workshop/seminar planner throughout the English-Speaking Caribbean and eventually a top-rated talk show host and opinion journalist on radio and for leading newspapers.

It was her passion for writing that drove her to establish **Yard Publications** in 1991, launching the "*Back A Yard*" series which was an annual satirical review of Jamaican politics. Six annuals were published before she decided to move on.

Her books currently active on Amazon are; *Looking Back, the struggle to preserve our freedoms, Talk Jamaican, Hidden Gems of Jamaica, Tour Jamaica* and *The Original Dancehall dictionary*."

For the kids too she also published; *The Original Jamaican Colouring Book; Count and Color; Draw and Color: Color and Learn*, all highlighting Jamaican scenes and lifestyles.

Up to her retirement in June 2016, she hosted ***"Joan Williams on Line"*** on Power 106 radio, which was broadcast worldwide. She also wrote a monthly column entitled **"*Enjoying the Jamaican Outdoors*"** for the Gleaner newspaper, highlighting places *off the beaten track* which she visited on her regular hikes and bicycle rides into the Jamaican countryside.

Joan is an active grandmother, a dedicated writer, a committed hiker, cyclist and outdoor lover and an accomplished artist.

She can be followed at; *http://joan-myviews.blogspot.com/* and contacted at *gratestj@gmail.com*

DEDICATION

This book is dedicated to all who have inspired me over the decades and contributed to my happiness, especially **Thor, Michele, Shadrach, Madelynn, Michelle and Bernard.**

It is also dedicated to all who will vote **in the USA in 2020**. May you make a wise decision, since what happens in **America affects the entire world.**

Another **Yard** Publication (September 2019)

Contact; <u>gratestj@gmail.com</u>

CONTENTS

INTRODUCTION

The price good men (people) pay for indifference to public affairs, is to be ruled by evil men. **Plato.**

Socialism is deplorable and *so is* **Racism**.

As I observe the various positions being put forward by politicians leading up to the 2020 presidential elections, I cannot but be concerned about what lies ahead, as what happens in the powerful USA, affects much of the world and especially countries like mine, *small and close to its shores.*

If some early news reports are to be believed, the choices that could be facing voters in that powerful country for those elections, would be broken down to **socialism** or **racism!**

In my book, the Republican party is totally racist, hence the title!

What a tragedy it would be if either of these two *evil philosophies* really became the only choices available in the USA.

While I suspect we all by now know *the iniquities of racism,* how many of the younger generation, especially those ages 18-24, (56% of whom a *Fox Poll* in February 2019 said *favor socialism,*) have any idea what that *dangerous* philosophy is all about?

Even many older Americans may be oblivious of how *toxic, farcical* and *unworkable* the *socialist economic model* really is, despite the regular depressing reports coming out of the once ultra-rich, liberal South American country of Venezuela.

I have relatives living in Cuba and have visited that country four times, so have first-hand information on how devastating socialism has been there too, both *financially* and *psychologically,* leaving the people *deprived, browbeaten* and *hopeless.*

I therefore have absolutely *no regrets* about the sacrifices *I personally* made in the mid-1970's, or that the party I supported, allegedly took *covert* assistance from the CIA to remove socialism from my small island of Jamaica.

While I had evidence that Cuban **DGI** and USSR's **KGB** were then directly involved in our affairs, I had no *concrete* evidence that the American CIA was. However, I believe they were, as that was during the *cold war era* when the superpowers meddled in almost every country, vying to spread their influence. So, **I** unequivocally thank

President Jimmy Carter, for authorizing that agency, to assist us to retain our freedoms and remove forever, the scourge of socialism.

For during that period, Cuba tried its best, in cooperation with our own democratically elected government at the time, to turn *Jamaica* into *a satellite socialist state.*

So grave was that danger, that not only did I have to take the *heart-wrenching* decision to send my young children away to safer shores, but also, I had to get on the frontlines at great personal danger, *dodging bullets* and *tear gas* as many courageous people are doing in Venezuela today.

Fortunately, from my observation, the real choices in the USA in 2020, will *not only* be *socialism* or *racism.*

Yes, there is a small, destructive socialist wing in the Democratic party that supports socialism.

One is led by Alexandria Ocasio-Cortez **(AOC),** who declared in March 2019, that *"Capitalism is irredeemable."*

The other socialist proponent is millionaire Bernie Sanders, who is seeking the democratic nomination.

He recently tried to disparage Elizabeth Warren by declaring she was a capitalist!

The fact is however, all other possible nominees for the Democratic party are capitalists, for only *would-be dictators* could support an economic model that stymies private initiative and puts the commanding heights of the economy under state control.

For state control of the economy proves to be so perilous everywhere it is tried, that unless people are *forced* to tolerate the consequences of that failed economic model, they inevitably reject it.

So, despite the propaganda aimed at painting the entire Democratic Party as socialist, nothing could be further from the truth, from what I have seen and heard.

Anyway, Americans have a third and better choice. That is, if the Democratic party does not blow it.

Let's think this through.

A **World Happiness Report** was developed in 2012, by the United Nations Sustainable Development Solutions Network, using global surveys to rank *156* countries by how *happy, their own citizens* perceive themselves to be.

Some factors considered are; economic wealth, life expectancy, social support, freedom to make life choices and levels of government corruption.

According to the 2019 report, the top ten countries where the happiest people on this planet live are; *Finland, Denmark, Norway, Iceland, the Netherlands, Switzerland, Sweden, New Zealand, Canada, Austria.*

The most powerful and richest country in the world, the USA, was way down at *number nineteen,* having fallen *five places* since the 2017 report was published.

Is this administration trying to frustrate the goal of *"pursuit of happiness"* set out in the Declaration of Independence?

Who could really be surprised that the happiness index would *decrease* in a country where health issues are the major cause of private bankruptcies?

Yet the Trump government is constantly threatening *to take away health care* from the poorest and most vulnerable, while cutting the taxes for the wealthiest!

According to Meik Wiking, CEO of think-tank The Happiness Research Institute in Copenhagen, Denmark, who took part in the report; "the erosion of happiness in the United States can be blamed on a "social crisis" where many Americans are increasingly feeling that they cannot trust their fellow citizens and feel "they have no one to count on in times of need." (Lack of safety nets, my interpretation.)

The divide between the rich and the poor is forever visible too in the USA, where approximately *3.5 million* men, women and children are homeless and living on the dangerous streets, while super rich, billion-dollar companies like Amazon and Google pay no federal taxes.

While such anomalies provide ammunition for opportunistic socialists, the fact remains that *the top ten countries* in The World Happiness Report 2019, are all *capitalist.*

Not one socialist country comes even in the top 90!

The top ten happiest countries have two things in common. They are; *necessary social programs* and equitable *regulatory policies* to prevent *predatory/unbridled capitalism.*

For when capitalism has no checks and balances, it inevitably causes the *majority* to be exploited by the *minority* wealthy/powerful individuals/companies.

My own analysis has revealed that the civilized and humane policies of the governments in those top ten happiest countries, are very much in sync with most what is being put forward by many of the politicians seeking to represent the Democratic party in the upcoming elections.

Does that not logically mean therefore that the *real* choices USA voters could face in 2020 are *socialism, racism* or *happiness,* making it so much wider than some political pundits are currently claiming?

Hopefully the Democrats will not make a hash of things and limit voters' choices.

Part 1
SOCIALISM

COMPARING SOCIALIST AND CAPITALIST ECONOMIES

The classic definition of socialism as set out by **Merriam Webster** is; *any of various economic and political theories advocating collective or governmental* **ownership** *and* **administration** *of the means of* **production** *and* **distribution** *of goods. (My emphases.)*

Disdain for this ideology is probably the only thing Donald Trump and I have in common. However, I doubt very much, that he really knows what socialism entails!

Without even seeing the proof on the ground, anyone who thinks through the definition above, should realize from the get go, how unworkable and inefficient a system would be, which leaves *production* and *distribution* of the resources to *politicians* and *bureaucrats*!

For when those critical elements are left to a handful of civil servants and opportunistic politicians opposed to *free market competition*, the natural outcome is *loss of productivity, corruption, nepotism, inefficiency,* and worst of all, *higher price* for consumers, as their choices are restricted or eliminated totally.

Consumers therefore become the big losers in a socialist economy.

This has been proven in every one of the numerous countries which declared *themselves socialist* between the 1960's and 1980's, when that philosophy was popular.

In the 1980's, before the notorious Berlin wall was demolished, thanks to Reagan and Gorbachev, I actually saw the stark contrast between *socialist* and *capitalist* countries many times. My most poignant memory however, was of East Germany which I visited twice during that period.

For driving from West Germany to the East during that period was like *going from the light into total darkness!*

Most of the numerous countries which adopted the backward socialist philosophy during the height of its popularity, were later forced to reverse those economic policies, *as citizens refused to continue enduring the suffering.*

Even a country like Vietnam, which I visited last year, though keeping the word "socialist" in its official name, (The Socialist Republic of Vietnam) is nothing close to being socialist these days.

I found the very opposite of socialism in Hanoi, as the city is bubbling with private enterprise activity everywhere, as capitalism is now firmly at the helm. On the other hand, I saw very little evidence of government involvement in *anything anywhere!*

China of course provides the greatest example of what happens when a country throws off the shackles of the *socialist economic system* and introduces capitalism, even gradually. Because for decades China wallowed in backwaters, with the equal distribution of *poverty*, seemingly being their most visible achievement.

However, just over forty years ago they started to liberalize their economy, got involved in world trade and allowed private enterprise to start taking over the productive process, and the county's economy has soared, with growth rates exceeding an average of 10% per year, for the last forty years.

China today is the *second wealthiest country in the world,* for they have liberalized their *economy* somewhat. They have not however eased restrictions on the rights of their citizens'. which is no doubt why they are way down at *number 93* in the 2019 World Happiness Report.

However, those countries which stubbornly maintain state control on the economy like Cuba, North Korea and latterly Venezuela, *remain almost unlivable.*

Venezuela, once the most vibrant, liberal democracy in South America, only declared itself socialist in 1998 but since then according to a United Nations report issued in May 2019, more than 4 million refugees and migrants have left the country, which is suffering from political *chaos, food shortages* and *hyperinflation.*

The U.N. has called this exodus the "largest in the recent history of Latin America and the Caribbean."

Jamaica too had a massive exodus in the 70's when our government experimented with socialism and it took decades for our economy to recover from that huge brain drain.

Each time I hear of socialism therefore, I never fail to silently thank all who helped us overcome that potential evil in Jamaica.

I freely admit that I was once a great proponent of the socialist system.

That was when I was a *youthful, naive, idealist* who, seeing the inequalities and suffering in my own country, eagerly swallowed socialism which was cloaked in the garb of 'equality and justice for all.'

It never took me long to find out however, that socialism in practice, is *a vicious, counter-productive, deplorable* and *unworkable system.*

A BRIEF HISTORY OF JAMAICA

The original inhabitants of the tiny Caribbean island now known as **Jamaica,** were the *Taino* Indians. The country has a total of land mass of only 10,990 square kilometers or 4,240 square miles,

They lived in some 200 villages spread all over the island, where they led quiet, peaceful lives as farmers, until all that was destroyed by the Spaniards after 1494, when Columbus accidentally landed at Rio Bueno on the north coast.

The island was then called *Xaymaca*, meaning *Land of Wood and Water*, but Columbus thought he would find gold there.

He was soon to find out however, that there was no gold anywhere in Jamaica.

As he needed wood and water and a chance to repair his vessels, he sailed west to *Discovery Bay,* where the Tainos had one of their better-established villages.

There he attacked the poorly armed natives *and claimed the island for Spain.*

The Spaniards who followed Columbus to their new prized holding, murdered or tortured and enslaved the Tainos and stole their land.

The process of the *almost total elimination* of the Tainos, was also aided by the introduction of European diseases to which the native people had little or no resistance.

Those left alive were so overworked and ill-treated that within a short time, most of the remaining indigenous people died.

As there was no gold, Jamaica served mainly as a supply base for the Spaniards, from which food, men, arms and horses were shipped to help in conquering the American mainland.

After Columbus' departure, little attention was paid to the colony by Spain and frequent attacks by British pirates also contributed to the colony's woes.

On May 10, 1655, the British led a successful attack on the island, causing the under-equipped Spaniards to quickly surrender, free their slaves, then most fled to Cuba.

The English settlers concentrated on using the island for growing crops on our fertile lands, that "mother country" needed. Sugar soon became the main produce, but it required a large number of field workers, to do the back-breaking work.

As Britain had from early in the fifteenth century started to invade Africa, it was there they went to capture thousands of poorly armed natives who they kidnapped, enslaved and brought to work on the island during the *cruel, genocidal Atlantic slave trade.*

To give you an idea of this brutal period in human trafficking, the first ship to be loaded with the humans in Africa for transportation to Jamaica was called **Hope**.

Its first cargo was made of 269 captured people of which *12% were children.* When it arrived in Jamaica, only 138 were still alive!

There were dozens of rebellions during that savage period of slavery, but these were violently and cold-bloodedly put down by the heavily armed British.

This brutal situation continued from 1655-1838 when slavery in the island was finally abolished, but Britain remained as our colonial masters.

During that period however, all the resources of the country continued to be *owned, controlled* and *enjoyed* by the British expatriate colonial masters, while the descendants of the slaves, who had by then become the majority, had little more than their physical strength.

The abolition of slavery therefore, did not leave the ex-slaves in any better condition, as with *no education, no land, no capital, no jobs,* nothing to start life with. So, after having been forcefully transported from Africa and laboring without compensation on British-owned plantations, they could barely survive.

On the other hand, the British government gave large cash compensations *to their nationals* who had been the slave owners, *for losing their serfs!*

A few fortunate ex-slaves were able to leave the island on rickety and unsafe canoes, in search of jobs overseas.

For the vast majority who could not escape, things became so desperate that *to stave off hunger and starvation,* most were forced to go back to work on the plantations run by the same brutal British land owners, who had worked them almost to death, under slavery.

That situation prevailed for numerous decades.

THE BIRTH OF OUR POLITICAL PARTIES

By the early nineteen hundred, conditions for plantation workers were so dire that a few trade unions started to be formed to give the oppressed laborers some leverage through *collective action*.

It was out of the growing, militant trade union movement that two major political parties were formed and they have alternated in government since independence in 1962.

These dominant parties are the *Peoples National Party (PNP)* which was formed in 1938 from the National Worker's Union (NWU), and the *Jamaica Labour Party (JLP)*, formed in 1943 out of the Bustamante Industrial Trade Union (BITU).

The PNP was then led by an attorney-at-law, Norman Manley and the JLP by trade unionist Alexander Bustamante.

They were cousins.

Both Bustamante and Manley were instrumental in agitating for self-government for the island.

Finally, we held our first general elections under *Universal Adult Suffrage*, in December 1944.

After three hundred years of British rule, on August 6, 1962, Jamaica finally gained its full independence from England, established a written constitution and adopted the Westminster Democratic system of government that their former colonial masters used in their own country.

In the early years after independence and continuing up to 1974, there was not much difference in the policies of the two major parties while they alternated in government, although the PNP had from time to time declared itself *socialist*.

Interestingly though, there was a significant difference in the makeup of the *core supporters* of the two parties, with the PNP garnering strong support from the powerful educated middle class. The JLP also drew some of their supporters from the upper classes, but the poorer manual workers supported them almost totally, because that party was attached to the *stronger and more vocal trade union*, the BITU.

A disturbing legacy from the centuries of the despicable British slave trade and colonial period of chronic racial discrimination, was the reality that black people were deprived of education so at independence, 42% were functionally illiterate.

Further, even many years after independence, most of the wealth of the nation was still owned and controlled by the British nationals and their descendants, some of whom were of mixed race.

The JLP government was elected to run the country immediately after we achieved independence. It concentrated on education, building elementary, high and technical institutions to educate those who were left behind during the period when the British ruled with an iron hand.

However, the ownership of much of the wealth of the nation continued to be held mainly in the *same hands* as it had been before.

This totally unjust situation provided a *populist platform* for the PNP, who seized the opportunity in their campaign leading up to the 1972 elections, to proclaim that they would promote *equal opportunity*, the *re-allocation* of resources and *social justice* for all.

MY OWN LIMITED BACKGROUND

Growing up in a tiny, sheltered, deep rural community in the former neglected British colony, I really had no idea how most Jamaicans lived, especially those in the crowded capital city of Kingston, for my home was in the village of Malvern in the south-western parish of St. Elizabeth, an area populated mainly by self-sufficient small farmers.

The usual picture was of each family having some land on which a home, though humble, would be built. The head of the household would cultivate the land around the house and whenever there was a bumper crop, vast improvements would be made to the house.

My father, though black, was a senior civil servant in the colonial government in the parish in which he was born, at a time when such positions were reserved for members of *the white expatriate British colonial elite.*

He was extremely brilliant and an accomplished technocrat and musician, but during the colonial era, that meant very little. I have therefore always suspected that he was only promoted up to the top job in the Collector of Taxes in the parish, the only institution he ever worked at after leaving high school, because the similar or *less qualified expatriates,* wanted to live *in the city* where they could access modern facilities, or on the *north coast* of the island, where there were beautiful, warm white-sand beaches close by.

You see, *our hilly parish* was totally out of the way, being over a hundred miles from the city, via mostly unpaved roads full of dangerous curves running alongside treacherous ravines.

As a result of my father's exalted position, I grew up in what I guess could be considered, middle class circumstances, attended a prestigious boarding school in the area and even learnt to drive in my teens, as my dad had one of the few cars in the area.

He however, did not like to drive to the city Kingston, as to him it was too crowded and fast moving. So, on the few occasions we went there, after a grueling four-hour drive, much to the disappointment of us kids, he would quickly conduct his business then return home immediately.

I couldn't wait to leave home to move to the city as my deep rural village, unlike Kingston, was dark, isolated and boring. So, on graduating from high school, I sought and got a job at a bank in the city then a year later, got an even better job at our only international airport.

Living with an aunt in the suburbs, I still saw or knew very little about most of the city, except of course the night clubs and nearby beaches.

On getting married two years later, my ex-husband and I migrated to *Toronto, Canada,* where we both had family living.

It was while there that I started to attend meetings of the *Jamaica-Canadian Association* and one night, was encouraged to go to what was being promoted as an exciting event. This, as our gathering would be addressed by none other than *the newly elected* and charismatic trade unionist and *Leader of the Opposition* in Jamaica, Michael Manley, who had succeeded his father as president of the PNP.

This was summer in the summer of 1970.

That meeting *changed my life forever*, for even now, I have rarely heard a more charismatic speaker than the late Michael Manley.

He was physically, an extremely imposing figure, standing much over six feet tall and with sharp, handsome features. From the minute he stated speaking, he held the total attention of his entire audience.

That was also the first time in my life that I heard first-hand about the intolerable level of poverty in our capital city Kingston, where it was estimated, between a quarter and a third of the island's population resided in overcrowded and unsanitary conditions.

I had never seen *a ghetto* when living in Jamaica, for as I said earlier, I grew up in the country and rarely visited the capital. When I worked in the city before migrating, I had no reason to visit those areas which were mainly downtown.

So, when Manley *graphically* described the miserable conditions under which thousands of people lived in abject poverty behind zinc fences, in small wooden shacks with several persons to one room and no bathroom facilities, I was genuinely shocked.

He blamed those conditions on the fact that the resources of the country were still concentrated in the hands *of the few descendants of the slave masters,* while the vast majority did not even have a tiny bit of land on which to grow food to feed their families.

More importantly, he blamed the governing party which had led Jamaica into independence and had run the country since then, for not having done *anything* to re-allocate the resources of the country. Thus, he emphasized, "that government had failed the people."

Manley also spoke passionately about the extremely high level of unemployment in some areas where persons could only stave off starvation, because of our unique practice known as, *running a boat.* This is a cooperative system which was handed down from the days of slavery, whereby daily, *communal meals* are cooked from the contributions of the very few who had anything at all.

These meager meals were then shared with *the many* who *had nothing.*

When he addressed the issue of unemployment, he also condemned the *evil system* being practiced by the government, where when job opportunities arose in the public service, only members of the ruling party were given the opportunity to apply.

He solemnly pledged that the government he led would *never practice victimization* against the Jamaican people.

When he had finished his address, I was the first person on my feet during the question and answerer session, asking how we Jamaicans in Canada could assist. His reply was immediate. *"Come home and help build your country."*

Without even thinking, my decision was immediate. I was going home.

HOMEWARD BOUND

I never had any difficulty convincing my ex-husband that we should return home and help build our country, for he too was not at all enamored by the cold climate and lack of good beaches in our adopted country. Two other young friends who attended the meeting, also assured us they would be returning home to fight for *justice for all the people*.

We decided to take the long way home by road, to see as much of North, Central and South America before we returned to settle down in Jamaica, as we had no idea when we would get an opportunity again to do so.

Fortunately, this was just about the time when the *Pan American Highway* was about to be completed. This highway was constructed to make travel easier from the United States to Panama.

As we had recently bought a cute little convertible British MG Midget sports car so we could enjoy the limited summer sunshine in Toronto, we decided to take it home, as Jamaica has year-round sunshine.

We therefore mapped a route through interesting cities in the USA, then on down to the newly opened highway. The plan was, once we reached

Panama, we would ship the car to Jamaica then use public transportation to continue our tour to South America, then go down the magnificent Amazon River by boat.

We did not give ourselves a timetable so decided that if we liked a place, we would hang around there for a while and where we didn't, we would move on.

So, packing a sleeping bag, a camping stove, a minimum of clothes and a tent, we set off on the road trip of our lives.

It was an exceptionally sunny September morn in 1970, when we kissed Toronto goodbye forever; then headed south.

It was an exciting and eventful journey through many United States cities until we made the mistake of going to Las Vegas, for there, immediately intoxicated by the bright lights, fantastic shows, air of excitement everywhere and most importantly, the sound of money loudly jingling all around in the casinos, we virtually lost our shirts and had to divert to California for a few weeks to work and replenish our funds.

I guess it is true that out of evil comes good, for that experience surely cured me from giving in to the lure of gambling *forever*. For although I have been back to Las Vegas quite a few times since then, as I love the ambiance and the shows and have visited other casinos in far flung places such as the Bahamas, Germany, St. Martin, St. Kitts, Monaco, Antigua and Atlantic City, I now only go to enjoy the entertainment but never take more than a maximum $10 with me into any of the casinos and when it is done it is done!

But back to the relevant narrative.

Leaving Las Vegas quickly, I was able to get a job immediately on arriving in Los Angeles, California, as I was proficient on the *unit record machine*, which is the precursor to the computer. My ex also got a job.

After working there for a few weeks, we headed for the Pan American highway, which went all the way to Panama but bypassed Belize.

We spent many memorable weeks in every country we visited in Central America but the only one that is relevant to this narrative was our visit to *El Salvador.*

This is because we got such a warm, remarkable reception there, simply because we came from a country close to Cuba! (Jamaica is only ninety miles away.)

When we were checking into the first hotel that we could afford there, we showed our passports as required, causing the clerk to be totally in the dark as to where Jamaica was.

In those days, the legendary *Bob Marley* had not yet had the international impact he now has, which had helped put us on the map worldwide. Neither had we yet produced a *Usain Bolt* who is still accepted by many, as the fastest man on the planet.

So, their lack of knowledge about our, little island, was understandable.

Our neighbor Cuba was however very dominant and their socialist revolution extremely popular in the region. Further, the revolutionary, *Che Guevara,* had been assassinated in Bolivia just a few years before and was regaled as a virtual martyr, in much of Latin America.

When we explained to the clerk that *Jamaica was Cuba's* closest neighbor, it was as if the messiah had landed!

I do not recall if it was a national holiday that was being celebrated there when we arrived, but there was a big party in the hotel that very night.

We were totally overcome during the festivities, therefore, when the master of ceremonies kept calling on us to stand up, as he introduced us, as the *"amigos from Jamaica."* Every time he mentioned Jamaica though, he explained to great applause, that it was located beside Cuba.

It was overwhelming.

When we arrived in Panama, we shipped our car to Jamaica and started to plan a route to Venezuela where my ex had an uncle living, who had invited us to spend some time with him before going home.

It was while checking out the boats that we heard about the beautiful beaches on the San Blas islands, and decided to divert a bit.

We soon found a vessel cooperatively owned by those Indians, which went to the islands.

This boat was used mainly to transport *their* people and supplies including food. At first, the captain was totally opposed to taking foreigners on as passengers, but he eventually relented.

The San Blas Islands are an archipelago comprising of 265 islands and cays but only 49 were inhabited. At that time, those islands were governed by Colombia although there was conflict with Panama over whose jurisdiction they should really fall under.

The inhabitants, apart from those who worked at the Panama Canal-zone, had very little exposure to outsiders except to fishermen and a few other persons coming from Colombia.

The people were extremely tiny in stature and I recall some even marveling at how tall I was for a woman. I also remember there being an over-abundance of albinos on most of the islands we visited. This was as a result of the popular practice of inter-marriages, we were told.

The women wore beautifully hand-woven clothes like what you see in Guatemala but the men were very scantily dressed, most times sporting nothing but a loin cloth. I was only able to take one picture with them during the long period we were there however, as according to their folk-lore, when you photograph them, you steal their souls!

The buildings on all the islands we visited were all made of thatch and sticks and the floors were simple warm, soft, white sand. These frail buildings were quite adequate on those islands however for although they are on the Caribbean coast, this region never has any hurricanes.

I don't think we would have left those islands for weeks as we were having such a wonderful time just hanging out on the cays and beaches, swimming and fishing.

Then, some nuns came over from Colombia to do health checks on the Indians. That was when we learnt that most of them suffered from *tuberculosis.*

That information of course caused instant panic, for we had been freely sharing utensils and living closely to them.

After roaming the beaches for a day, we finally found a fisherman who agreed to take us on his tiny boat to Colombia. We spent a few days in that country, then used public transportation to go over to Venezuela where our relative worked.

He lived in *Maracaibo,* the second largest city in the country after Caracas.

Unlike today, Venezuela was then *a prosperous liberal democracy* with a high standard of living, exceeding any I had seen anywhere outside of the USA or Canada.

Our relative worked in the oil industry there, as did hundreds of other foreigners. He gave us a wonderful vacation, taking us on tours and to restaurants all over.

It was with real regret that we had to leave Venezuela, and that is partly why I find it *so* painful to see the depths of despair, into which *socialism* has dragged that country today.

SOCIALISM: HOGWASH AND HYPOCRISY

When I returned to Jamaica in January 1971, I was pregnant but as soon as I could, I got involved in political activity, joining the *PNP Youth Organization* (PNPYO*)*, plus a small local *group* in the community that we lived.

The *group* was the arm of the party which worked with grassroot supporters, teaching them what the *party line* was on every issue, while instructing them to find out, *the party affiliation of every one of their neighbors*.

This was a critical party function that each group member had, for where neighbors shared the same party affiliation, the group member had to ensure that they were registered to vote. Where the neighbor was uncommitted or supported the other party, the group member had a duty to try to convince him/her that the PNP was the best choice for the country.

The PNPYO was the militant arm of the party, organizing and participating in street demonstrations.

In 1971, there were two hot button issues at the top of the list of the opposition PNP, which were consuming the energies of the party leaders.

These were the *Lottery Debate* and the *disenfranchising* of young voters.

During the late 1960's, the JLP government had introduced a national lottery which was almost universally welcomed, because it created hundreds of jobs for poor unemployed people who could earn a commission for selling these tickets everywhere, including on the open sidewalks or in the streets.

The profit raised from the lottery, was dedicated to fixing and maintaining the public hospitals which were in terrible condition, as there was just not enough tax revenue coming into the government coffers, to deal with the myriad of health issues.

However, most churches, even those involved in fund-raising activities where bingo was played, were vehemently opposed to the lottery, as they claimed that it was gambling and gambling was *evil* and *unchristian-like*.

This led to a heated debate in a country where some *95%* of the population describe themselves as being Christian!

Recognizing the great influence of the clergy, Manley, the opposition leader, who was a master tactician, immediately sided with them to get the attention of the churchgoers. He also succeeded in convincing a horde of young, idealistic persons including me, that despite the good that the profits from the lottery were doing for the poor, it had to go, *as gambling was sinful.*

Almost weekly, the streets were full of clergymen in their religious garb, marching around with placards, behind members of the executive of the Jamaica Council of Churches (JCC). Naturally, thousands of us young, exuberant, *newly-converted* placard-bearing, activists soon joined them, shouting about the evils of gambling.

We had no compunction about telling curious on-lookers that a country could not prosper, if it accepted tainted funds, for the ends just could not justify the means!

Of note is the fact that Jamaica today, has an active lottery industry which is operated for *personal profit.* For eventually a license to operate a private lottery was awarded *to a large financial backer* of the same party which had fought so fiercely against the *publicly-run* National Lottery which was financing the hospitals. The Jamaica Council of Churches remained very silent on that *turn-*

around and the general public who love to gamble plus those who can earn an income selling the lottery, welcomed the move!

The subject of *disenfranchisement* had become topical, because the ruling JLP government recognized that with the new leadership of the younger Manley in the PNP, the youth were being attracted to his party in droves.

So, they had to do something about it.

Someone in the government therefore came up with the brilliant idea *of stopping the registration of voters,* two full years before new elections were constitutionally due. (General elections are constitutionally due *every five years,* although the Prime Minister has the sole authority to determine the actual date within the given period.)

There was no computerization of the system then, so the voter registration process could be long and tedious. However, they could have kept registration centers open longer, so people could go in whenever they could. Instead, the government closed everything down, long before necessary, thus disenfranchising those who attained the voting age *up to two years before* the election was called.

Although I was over the voting age, I too was disenfranchised as I could not be registered although I arrived in the island more than a year before the elections were held.

Disenfranchisement therefore, was particularly offensive to me. So, I don't recall a street demonstration against that issue ever taking place, in which I was not deeply involved in some way, even if it was only to paint placards.

The PNP easily won the 1972 general elections, mainly due to the overwhelming support they received from young people.

One of the first things they did, was to set up a party organization aimed mainly at young professionals, called the "*Task Force.*" It was considered so important that it fell under the chairmanship of a full cabinet minister.

This body was assigned to the recruit suitably qualified young people to work in the government service.

Naturally, I joined immediately, as remember, the whole idea of my returning home was to help to "build my country."

Soon, it was evident however, that if one didn't subscribe to "*democratic socialism,*" the means by which we were told, *social justice was to become a reality in Jamaica,* one could not qualify to work in the public service.

Further, task force members who already worked in the government service were required to bring to meetings, a list of names of persons working in their department, who they either *knew* or *suspected*, did not support the ruling party.

When I heard about this at my first meeting, it made me very uncomfortable as I remembered clearly, how Manley at the meeting in Canada, had described that same process as "political victimization," an evil being practiced by the previous government, and vowed at the time, that no party *he* led would ever do something like that.

However, my question on the topic was answered tersely by the chairman, who explained that if they did not have committed people who subscribed to the party's philosophies working in the establishment, government policies could be *sabotaged.*

Throwing principles aside, I accepted the justification immediately!

You see, on my return to Jamaica, I had really become so fanatical, that anything Manley or his cohorts even suggested, I *swallowed* and *followed* unthinkingly.

Even when they exhorted us to shun imported products to help save the country's limited foreign exchange and keep the jobs at home, I immediately started eating and drinking everything local, throwing out things like even good Canadian whiskey, (rye) for which I had developed quite a liking!

This naïve stance of mine continued until I realized that what the leadership of the PNP was telling us was sheer, *unadulterated hogwash* and *hypocrisy*.

For soon, the free press, ran a series of exposures on what was being consumed at events being hosted by members of the hierarchy of the government. Not only did the stories detail the menus, which were inevitably full of *imported luxury dishes* and *liquors*, but we also discovered too, that the furnishings in their homes and offices were all lavish and imported.

This while the government was vociferously charging the population, via a myriad of media ads, to use local products.

I also confirmed this double standard for myself not too long after, on attending a party that a minister hosted for his girlfriend. Did the imported champagne flow ever so freely there, while there was a never-ending supply of caviar!

A similar pattern between how the "privileged" lived as opposed to the "masses," also emerged in the so-called *re-allocation of resources.*

Under specially designed programs, the government targeted huge acreages of land which were owned by a handful of people. Even where those properties were in full production, they declared that they would acquire the land from those owners, subdivide them into smaller parcels, and re-allocate sections to small farmers, so thousands of landless people could benefit.

What happened in practice though, was that the wealthy land owners who supported the governing party, could keep their properties unhindered, while they forcefully "bought" the lands from the others at a price determined by the government, which paid for it, many years later.

Worse, most of these lands, once acquired, were subdivided and allocated *to party supporters only.*

In most instances, these new land barons had absolutely no interest in farming or any plan to keep or put the lands into production.

Some of the farms which were in full production, were ravaged as the new owners sold off or consumed the cattle and crops, but *no restocking or replanting* was ever done.

As the Bank of Jamaica had already started to reduce the allocation of foreign exchange to food importers, as part of the *eat Jamaica* campaign, the loss of the products previously supplied from thousands of acres of *once productive* farms, was the genesis of the food shortages which became the norm in Jamaica, for the first time since the World War 11.

RETHINKING POLITICS

I had a second child in 1973, and my flirtation with the PNP government, lasted for about four years after I had returned to Jamaica and had eagerly and unthinkingly embraced "Democratic Socialism." However, when the writing started to appear on the wall that the high ideals they held up while in opposition were only a *sham*, I stopped attending party meetings and became openly leery of the PNP.

However, I never contemplated ever joining the opposition party, whose leader, Edward Seaga, I considered *dictatorial, unattractive* and *undesirable* in many ways.

So, I resigned myself to removing political activism from my life and concentering entirely on earning a living and looking after my young children.

Soon, the party's total rejection of the *"democratic"* label in their new found socialist philosophy, became more evident daily.

As I stated earlier, Jamaica lies only ninety miles south of Cuba and there have been long-standing ties between people in both countries. This, because from the late 19th to the early 20th century, when the thousands of the slaves and their descendants, could make little economic progress at home, nearby Cuba became the place to go. This was because that island had a booming economy, based mainly on their thriving sugar cane industry.

Thousands of Jamaicans including close relatives of mine, therefore migrated there to take advantage of employment opportunities.

Cuba had always been run by dictators, but none more brutal than *Batista*, who seized power in a bloodless coup in 1952.

He not only suppressed all dissent by controlling the university, the press, and the Congress, but also embezzled huge sums from the booming economy. He also turned Cuba into the playground for rich Americans, including notorious organized crime figures and members of the mafia.

He also had the full endorsement and support of successive American governments.

In 1959, he was overthrown by a band of popular revolutionaries led by *Fidel Castro*. After being rebuffed by the Americans, Castro seized all private property including many owned by Americans and turned Cuba into a satellite of the powerful Soviet Union. (*USSR.*)

Readers will recall that during that *cold war era,* the USSR and USA were in stiff competition *for world domination.*

Our prime minister Michael Manley, met the charismatic Fidel Castro at a Non-aligned conference in 1974. Once he became exposed to the *supreme power* Castro wielded unhampered in his island, Manley decided that he needed to adopt that type of government but keep the "*democratic*" label when selling the new philosophy to Jamaicans.

Because we Jamaicans tend to be generally kind and caring people, which is what the *democratic socialist package* at first implied it would promote, (social justice,) Manley's initial message got overwhelming support from almost every sector in the entire nation.

What he did not take into consideration however, was the fact that because we were close to both *Cuba* and *America*, the general population was totally knowledgeable about both systems of government.

So, when he later tried to *surreptitiously* introduce Cuban-style totalitarianism into Jamaica, the direct threat this would pose to *press freedom* and the *democratic process to which we were accustomed,* was immediately recognized and resisted.

CUBA AND RUSSIA IN
THE 70'S

For the benefit of those born after the 80's, I must reiterate that Cuba and Russia are not *today,* what they were then.

During that period, the USSR Empire which was dominated by Russia, was extremely powerful with numerous satellite-states worldwide. All were controlled and dominated by the iron hand of the huge, brutal USSR military machinery and the KGB, with local stooges in every satellite country. (After the USSR broke up and Russia emerged as a world power, the name of the KGB was changed to **FSB**, the same spy agency which was so involved in the USA's 2016 presidential elections.)

The USSR had no reservations about foisting their totalitarian system on other countries, using *the bullet* whenever and wherever they could get a toehold.

Cuba, as its western regional satellite, saw the small vulnerable Caribbean islands as easy pickings, especially if it could get influential local people or organizations like Manley's PNP in *Jamaica* and the New Jewel Movement in

Grenada, to become their surrogates and open the doors.

As the Jamaican proxies drew closer to the Cubans, numerous Cuban soldiers were deployed into Jamaica (and Grenada as well, we later learnt) and spread out island-wide, under the guise that they were building mini-dams and schools for us.

In Jamaica, the PNP government also recruited young men, mainly from their party's youth arm, who were sent to Cuba, supposedly to be trained in work-related skills.

Instead they were trained in *guerilla warfare.*

One defector from the program exposed it all in a book published in the 70's entitled "*The Road Not Taken.*" (It is still available on Amazon).

The Cuban assistance to the PNP did not stop there however, as that country also provided wanted gunmen affiliated to the ruling party, with a haven in which to remain until the local heat had worn off.

A notorious case was that of two men named *Tony Brown and George Flash,* who were wanted for murder by the local police. Details of the sordid affair, involving their being given refuge in Cuba and their return to Jamaica *twenty years later,* by which time witnesses and files had disappeared, can be found in the archives of our leading newspaper, the daily Gleaner.

During the mid-seventies, when hordes of Cuban soldiers entered our island, they were visible in almost every community, traversing our streets in open-back trucks under the guise that they were volunteer construction workers. However, their presence and activities became extremely intimidating.

Soon the free press and many of us who were uncomfortable with their presence, started to openly criticise their existence and question their real motives.

This caused the Cuban ambassador to Jamaica Ulysses Estrada, a former General in the Cuban army, to commandeer time on our national television station which was at the time owned by the government.

There he delivered a blistering broadcast in which he brazenly warned *us* Jamaicans, that if we did not cease our criticism of the presence of Cubans in the island, he would ***"Bring in his army to deal with us."***

While many Jamaicans had previously been silent about the growing Cuban influence and presence in the island, Estrada's menacing threat caused most of us freedom-loving people to decide that, after centuries of British colonialism and slavery, we would not be allowing our newly won independence to be wrested away from us *by Cubans*.

Another sign that the country was heading on a dangerous path, was the promotion of *hate-filled* rhetoric by senior members of the government, using the government-owned radio and television stations, along with the Daily News, a state-run newspaper, to spread their divisive message. These messages were usually about the *"evils of capitalism"* and to blame the private sector for the growing food shortages.

Simultaneously with the closer embrace of the Cubans, came open verbal and sometimes physical attacks on people who appeared to be wealthy or who openly disagreed with the government.

They were labeled as being *wicked rapacious exploiters* or *stooges of the Americans*.

After a while, even driving on the streets, I soon became accustomed to hearing people shouting *"wicked rapacious capitalist"* at me, simply because I drove a car!

LEGITIMIZING THEFT

Also popular under our socialist experiment, was the *open promotion of stealing*, of not only farmer's crops and people's private possessions, but also land.

The *justification* for this campaign was propaganda spewed out to the effect that whoever had any form of wealth, had inherited it from the wicked colonial masters, so it was *justice* for it be taken from them.

It was therefore implied that theft would be redefined as *capturing,* which now meant *necessary action to reallocate the resources of the nation*!

A few years after we returned home to Jamaica, as my ex and I had both always dreamt of becoming farmers, we had mortgaged everything we owned to pay down on a hundred-acre property in St. Catherine, which is the adjoining parish south of the city.

By then, I had been making my displeasure with the direction the government was taking, publicly known by frequently writing "*letters to the editor*" which the only independent newspaper, the daily Gleaner, eagerly published. This was not because I knew anyone at the publication or was in any way a celebrity, but most people were so *intimidated* by the government that they were afraid to express their views openly.

So since, the newspaper was getting very few letters of criticism to balance those of praise that persons who wanted to ingratiate themselves with the government were sending in, mine were often published.

Being a small society, our farm was quickly targeted by people charging that we were supporting the opposition and wanted the government to fail. They then started to brazenly invade our property to take whatever they could extract, declaring that they were "capturing" our things as we were "wicked capitalists."

With political animosity increasing and destructive rhetoric being tossed around at persons who were not socialists, it was only a matter of time before, people with few resources but lots of ambition, initiative and skill, joined their wealthier counterparts to migrate from Jamaica in droves, taking their assets and skills with them.

That is mainly why you find such large Jamaican communities in nearby Florida, for as Jamaicans fled from socialism, they sought a place with compatible weather.

Interestingly, although quite a number of Jamaicans who claimed they were socialists also fled as the economy deteriorated, *I have never* met or seen any of the socialists that I knew, living in Cuba on my many trips there. However, I am forever meeting or reconnecting with them in capitalist Florida!

THE FINANCIAL CRUNCH INTENSIFIES

As the cold war rhetoric inspired by obedience to Russia/Cuba escalated, it also targeted visitors to our island, especially those identified by their accents as "American imperialists." At the time, tourist from America made up 75% of our visitors.

It was not surprising therefore, that during that period, tourism also floundered, so our GDP declined sharply and increasingly, hard currency, became unavailable.

As foreign exchange became scarcer, the Jamaican dollar constantly devalued and the black market flourished. The natural result of this economic turmoil was; price increases, food shortages, frequent power cuts, and high inflation.

I remember all too well, the regular power cuts during that dark era, as the government could not afford to buy even oil to keep the generators at the publicly-owned power company rolling. I also remember having to line up on alternating days to be allowed the *luxury* of buying fuel for my vehicle and of course the chaos and frustration of having to fight to get a place in the long lines to buy basic foods, similar to what is reported to be happening in Venezuela today.

While we the masses suffered however, there were frequent news reports in the independent newspaper about the opulence being flaunted by the politicians, their cohorts and relatives.

Worse, as the factory operators and other business owners could not get foreign exchange to import necessary inputs and goods to keep their establishments afloat, joblessness increased exponentially.

The government's only answer to the shortage of hard currency, was to institute *heavy-handed* exchange controls which *criminalized* anyone caught trying to leave the island or having in their possession, more than US $50!

As always happens when the movement of money anywhere in the world is restricted, more innovative means are found to manipulate the system and hide funds.

In our case, to enforce the new measures and prosecute those taking out their *own money* from the country, the government established a body called the *Financial Intelligence Unit*, (the FIU) but soon bribery won the day and the agents there became the main conduits through which the money was safely taken on board the outgoing planes!

I understand that most agents at that institution became super rich during that period.

By the mid 70's, the US press started to take a keen interest in the anti-American taunts tourists returning home were reporting that they faced on the streets in one of their favorite Caribbean destinations. When the additional information about the shortage of basic items in the hotels was added, the entire tourism industry, the chief earner of foreign exchange, took a direct hit.

With the blossoming of jobless people on the streets, came an increase in persons who were directly motivated to express their disaffection with the government through regular demonstrations.

It wasn't only shortages, joblessness, power cuts, verbal vitriol etc. which escalated during that period of economic decline therefore, but also frequent demonstrations and violence born out of frustration.

In no time what started as community-based demonstrations often spread nationally. As they did, the government mobilized its supporters, including those who had been trained in guerrilla tactics in Cuba, to violently put down these protests.

The political opposition, seeing how the growing dis-satisfaction with government policies was driving ordinary people to the streets, joined in and encouraged *their* activists to get involved in the demonstrations.

Quickly, many parts of the island became consumed by violence resulting in deaths and injuries which made the daily news reports extremely alarming.

By 1976, these limited street activity rapidly escalated into a fully blown *undeclared civil war* between PNP and JLP supporters who mysteriously graduated overnight, from using stones, knives and handguns to AK 47's, Uzis and M16's, allegedly supplied to the PNP by the Cuban DGI and USSR KGB and to the JLP by the American CIA.

I had become totally disenchanted with the PNP government by about mid-1975, but because I did not like what I heard about Edward Seaga, the newly elected leader of the JIP, I never considered getting involved with the opposition party.

So, I continued to write my critical letters to the editor *or* join a few community-based demonstrations when I couldn't find basic goods in Spanish Town, but tried to distance myself from the political parties.

However, a few months before the general elections of 1976, the Manley government implemented a most dangerous and oppressive law, that demonstrated beyond all reasonable doubt that they were setting out to implement a Cuban-style regime in Jamaica.

THE POLITICAL STATE OF EMERGENCY

On Saturday 19th June, 1976, Prime Minister Michael Manley, told parliament that his government would be implementing a State of Emergency, with the reasons stated as:

a) To reduce crime and to apprehend the gunmen and the new breed of terrorist;

b) To smash the link between politics and violence;

c) To give the nation a breathing space to return to normality;

d) To create an atmosphere of security conducive to the effective functioning of the economy;

e) To permit Law abiding citizens comprising of the overwhelming majority of our population, to pursue without fear their peaceable business in homes, work-places or in the streets and public places.

(Source: Library at the Institute of Jamaica.)

While all that sounded lofty enough, instead of the State of Emergency being used for the purposes legislated and announced, *it soon became an instrument to lock up influential opposition activists.*

Politically aligned police were sent out in full force to immediately arrest without charge and place in *indefinite detention*, well known JLP leaders and supporters all over the island.

Those detained were then herded into cramped detention centres under the most inhumane conditions.

But not only were political adherents being arrested without charge but also it was often reported, that police who had personal beefs against individuals, used the *blank* detention orders which had been pre-signed by the Minister of Security and given out at random, to deal with their enemies too!

Prime Minister Manley insisted at the time when 1976 State of Emergency was declared, that it was the government's initiative to deal with the escalation in violence, *as recommended by his security advisors.*

That was later exposed as a flagrant lie at a Commission of Enquiry held in 1978, called the *Smith Commission*, which was chaired by the then Chief Justice of Jamaica Hon. Kenneth Smith.

The report of that enquiry revealed in part that; "its calling was predicated upon the facilitation of *political opportunism* and not bona fide concerns about national security."

The Smith Commission also found that the head of both intelligence agencies of government -- the Special Branch of the police force and the Military Intelligence Unit (MIU) of the Jamaica Defense Force -- never advised Manley of any potential threat to national security during Carifesta (Caribbean Cultural Festival) and, indeed, Deputy Commissioner Curtis Griffiths, head of the Special Branch, testified to the commission that he knew nothing about the intention to declare a State of Emergency; he read of it in the press, although he was the chief intelligence officer of government. Captain Carl Marsh, in charge of the MIU also gave devastating testimony. He advised that there was no need for a State of Emergency."

Soon after that State of Emergency was declared, but before the commission of enquiry was set up, I recognized from the actions of the government, that it was nothing but a political tool to give the Manley government supreme power over us, as existed in Cuba. I therefore, decided that despite what I had been hearing about Seaga's dictatorial leadership style, because he was the leader of the only *viable alternative party*, I would have to join the JLP.

For Russian/Cuban domination of my country was totally unacceptable to me.

I therefore volunteered, to assist in any way I could, the JLP representative who was running in my constituency.

Incidentally, switching from PNP to JLP, opened my naive eyes for the first time, to how *cultish* even very educated persons were, when it came to politics, always putting the interest of their party over that of the country. For I had a very good friend at high school with whom I had reconnected in the PNPYO. We then started to travel together all over the city and even to neighboring parishes to attend PNP meetings. We collaborated closely on most things, not only political but private matters as well. I was therefore really shocked and hurt at how he took my switch in party allegiance, for to me *he was a friend*. But as soon as it became known in party circles that I was campaigning for the JLP, I can still see the raw hatred in his eyes as he glared at me, turned his back and walked away, the first time I saw him after my transition.

I have since come to accept that this is how politics generally is, not only in Jamaica but also all over the world!

In retrospect, I was lucky that the only adverse reaction I had to my move was a snub from a close friend, for in Jamaica at that time, and in many countries throughout the world, such acts of *betrayal* are considered a good reason for assassination!

To Trump, we saw how the changing of allegiance by Michael Cohen was considered so despicable, that it gave the President good reason to publicly brand him as a "rat," with all its implications in mafia lingo!

The JLP had no chance of winning the 1976 general election because numerous representatives, organizers and senior leaders and even some influential supporters in small communities, were being locked up or had to go into hiding.

The most senior political leader who was detained without charge, was one Pernell Charles, then the deputy leader of the JLP and a Vice President of the affiliated trade union, the BITU.

His entire family had to flee and seek asylum in the USA where his wife was later involved in a car accident which had her placed-on life-support. However, the government *would not allow him to travel abroad*, even in handcuffs, to visit his dying wife and young children.

He later wrote a memoir entitled "*Detained*" in which he vividly recorded his experiences during that terrifying period when he was detained in the most inhumane conditions, for *an entire year.*

If after months of blatant and undemocratic detention of opposition figures, the breaking up their meetings, the pursuing and terrorizing of their supporters at every level by the politically aligned members of the security forces, any doubt remained in anyone's mind what the real purpose of the State of Emergency was, all doubt was removed on election day.

A good example was when Karram Josephs, the JLP's caretaker for probably the most peaceful constituency in the island, North East Westmoreland, was arrested.

Not one shot had been fired in that constituency or one incident of violence reported during the entire election period, but Josephs was detained at *7 am* on election morning, because he was said to be a ***threat to national security***. Amazingly, that threat to national security disappeared *at 6 pm* the same evening when the polls closed. He was then released without explanation, for clearly that was the hour he ceased being a threat!

Other less well-known opposition leaders and activists in every constituency suffered a similar fate.

The PNP "won" 47 of the 60 seats in that election.

OUTWARD MIGRATION
ESCALATES

After the results started to sink in, the flight of terrified Jamaicans, taking with them whatever assets they could, intensified. Many sold their properties for a song, as the government was threatening to escalate the nationalization of private properties across the island.

Several large businesses and farms were immediately nationalized and turned into *peoples' cooperatives* with huge numbers of "socialists" settling on these as the proud new owners.

In no time though, the new owners sold off or devoured all the livestock and other farm products.

With no one replacing anything, those once-productive farms were soon left in ruins.

In addition to the nationalisation drive, there was also increased *state terrorism* which further propelled the flight of the middleclass, business-persons and indeed anyone who could find a place of refuge or simply just leave Jamaica for *anywhere.*

While most had become accustomed to being vilified on the streets as being *rapacious capitalists* due to, for example, no other reason but owning and driving a motor vehicle, the escalating threats of physical violence or arrest without charge, simply became too much for them.

Simultaneously, those in the hierarchy of the socialist movement who were intent on grabbing state power and resources, soon became dissatisfied with using threats alone. So immediately as the party was re-elected, actions designed to drive terror into the hearts of those who swore they would never abandon their country but refused to endorse democratic socialism, were put into place.

These included the wide-scale burning down of the homes of dissenters; threats of detention under the State of Emergency and direct unprovoked acts of violence against innocent family members.

Rape too, became a weapon used to terrorise, especially the middle class as they were the most publicly vocal against the Manley regime.

Reports abounded about children, some as young as three years of age, being raped as their helpless parents were forced to watch, some horror stories revealed.

It was a terrible, chilling, dangerous and blood-curdling period and the outward flight of the professionals and entrepreneurs swelled to a deluge to the point where some streets in middle class areas, were reportedly blocked by trailers as people hurried to flee the island with their belongings and families.

Interestingly though, some of the millionaires and billionaires in Jamaica today, are members or relatives of the ruling political elite that dominated the island at that time, preaching about the evils of capitalism and wealth accumulation. For as happened in the USSR after the fall of the Berlin wall, the former socialists in Jamaica, seized control of much of our national assets for very little money or sometimes for nothing.

During those terrible 1970's, most of my friends and acquaintances, were completely panic-stricken and quickly joined the horde who fled to safer shores in North America. In retrospect, I think the only reason why my young family and I did not join the exodus, is because we had only recently returned home and started to re-discover the *incomparable* beauty of our homeland,

Leaving it to be destroyed by political thugs therefore, was just not a palatable option for us.

We tried to stay busy, attempting to make a success of our excessively-mortgaged farm in St. Catherine.

While my ex-husband concentrated on planting rice on the largest section of the farm, I was always interested in livestock farming and wanted to give that a try.

Not having much money to buy animals, I prepared a business plan to operate a dairy on the rest of the land, using the feedstock method instead of open range.

I then applied to the government-operated Agricultural Credit Bank (ACB) for a loan and was extremely excited when an officer visited the farm, looked over the facilities and the proposal and assured me they would have no problem financing the project.

Then he dropped the bombshell.

To get the project passed and the loan approved, I would have to give him *a kickback of 20%* of the principal that I wanted to borrow!

Of course, there was no one I could report him to, as most persons employed by the government agencies, were highly *accredited party people,* who could only gain employment after meeting the conditions of the *party's Task Force!* (Remember, the primary function of that body which I once was a member of, was to guarantee the *political purity* of persons being employed in the government service. *Integrity* or *competence* had no influence there!)

Without the capital that the loan would have provided, I was limited to go into minor egg production with only around 200 chickens.

Then disaster struck, as one morning I went to feed my precious hens, only to find my poultry house *totally empty*. My entire capital outlay had clearly been "captured," by people who considered it appropriate treatment for *wicked capitalists*.

That put paid to my intentions to continue farming as I had no money to restock.

The good thing though was that rice could not be stolen as it could only be economically reaped mechanically, as we discovered the hard way.

Up to before the mass migration, there had been one rice combine in the entire parish of St. Catherine, where rice production was extensive.

That one combine, had *effectively* reaped the rice on all the huge plantations there, for years.

Like so many other persons who were fleeing Jamaica at the time however, the owner of the reaper decided to move to Belize, in Central America, taking his equipment with him.

To fill the gap, a government agency, the Agricultural Development Corporation (ADC), bought *four* rice reapers from the USSR to replace the *one* that had done the job before.

But would you believe that when a farmer wanted the use of the equipment, none could be acquired!

For true to form, when government operates anything, there is nothing but massive inefficiency and other problems, including outright corruption.

So those reapers which were already very inferior to the privately-owned one made in the USA, were not being properly maintained. Besides, they had no spare parts for them, as either many workers got involved in the "national past-time" of stealing (capturing!) everything that was not nailed down or there was no foreign exchange available to import the parts.

Soon therefore, all the reapers were scrapped, thus putting them permanently out of commission.

That was the beginning of the end of rice production in the entire parish of St. Catherine and today I do not think you can find a grain of rice there!

I remember our last crop vividly, for when the rice was ready to be reaped, we could not find a reaper to rent. In desperation, we even tried the impossible, seeking out labourers from near and far, to try and accomplish the expensive, frustrating and laborious task of reaping some 30 acres by hand.

We had to give up after a day or two however and accept the fact that we had been totally wiped out financially. For trying to reap that amount of rice by hand would have cost us at least three times more than what *we would earn* selling the product to the mill.

JUMPING INTO POLITICS HEAD FIRST

With nothing more to lose financially, I became more involved in political activity, for despite being terrorized, having his key organizers detained under the State of Emergency and recently losing the 1976 elections, Seaga, the leader of the opposition JLP, seemed to have become invigorated and decided to fight back.

Having learnt a great deal about political organizing when I was a member of the PNP, I established a local JLP branch in my community, to mobilize at the grassroots. I also started to visit the JLP headquarters in Kingston as often as I could, to see how I could help with anything.

As petroleum was being rationed, I was happy that I had a small bike, a Suzuki 50, which I could afford to use to travel the twelve miles each way to the city.

I also joined into every demonstration I heard about. Naturally, the political police and political goons always arrived at these events, to break them up as quickly as possible.

On one occasion, as I was demonstrating in Spanish Town and handing out pamphlets, a *senior superintendent* of police, even confiscated my package of anti-government pamphlets and ordered them destroyed!

However, even before that event, I had begun to develop a total dislike and distrust for members of our security forces, not only because they had become blatantly politicised after the State of Emergency and been using their awesome powers to lock up and terrorize non-socialists without cause and tear gassing us whenever we gathered to demonstrate, but also, I had even been recently locked up by one in a most unfair situation.

I had taken my mom to a funeral in the mid-island parish of Clarendon where she was born, and afterward had driven her to my childhood home where she still lived.

I left Malvern for my home in Kingston which is almost a hundred miles away, at about *4 am* the next morning.

In the mid-island town of Mandeville, I stopped at the only traffic light they had there at that time, as it was red. However, as crime was escalating and people were often being attacked by criminals at lonely intersections after dark, I wasn't about to take any chances even in supposedly peaceful Mandeville. So, when I saw no other cars around at the intersection, I drove off before the light changed to green.

I hadn't seen the police car parked at the petrol station nearby, so was really surprised when I heard a siren behind me. Thinking he was going to a crime scene I did not stop immediately.

When the cop caught up with me, I stopped. He jumped out his vehicle and aggressively approached my window, gun drawn. I was extremely scared as I smelled that he was *reeking of stale rum.* Immediately, he started to verbally abuse me severely, interspersing his diatribe with curse words.

Angrily I threw back at him a few of the choice bad words he had told me, only to have him react by pointing the gun at my head and dragging me off to jail in the town.

So really, I had come to expect nothing but harassment, tear gassing and unpleasant interaction with the police.

THE CIVIL WAR ESCALATES

By 1977, the brutal undeclared civil war escalated, and the death toll rose exponentially.

I am still convinced that had that State of Emergency been really used to ferret out the gunmen from *both parties*, instead of just being an instrument to intimidate and detain JLP activists and supporters, Jamaica would never have descended to the level of violence that prevailed then and to some extent, which still affects our small island up to today.

Because as the 1976 State of Emergency was being misused to deprive people of their rights and all basic items were becoming scarcer each day, open warfare in many communities became commonplace.

Apart from the hundreds of people being seriously injured or killed in political battles, there were numerous families being left homeless, as the burning of the houses of political rivals became somewhat of a past-time among many activists.

I do not think *any* of our fourteen parishes was left unscathed, though maybe the residents were not living in fear to the extent that most in the capital city were.

Not even the police were safe as there were frequent assaults on their stations.

It was the children who were affected most though, as schools in volatile areas had to be closed frequently due to the regular pitched battles within earshot.

Even if the schools were not closed, absenteeism born of fear, became frequent.

Additionally, when the children attended schools in the war-torn areas, they had difficulty concentrating because of the constant gunfire and mayhem.

The hospitals, already short of drugs, nurses, doctors and basic equipment due to migration and the foreign exchange shortage, also became overwhelmed.

There were some especially gruesome atrocities being committed by both sides, in the name of politics, the likes of which had never been heard of before in the English-Speaking Caribbean.

Some were so frightfully blood-curdling or downright treacherous, that I must mention them.

The four that will forever remain entrenched in my memory are; the *Orange Lane Fire,* the *Green Bay Massacre,* the *Gold Street Massacre* and *the*

Moonex Affair which involved a case of high treason.

The Orange Lane Fire

On May 19, 1976 ten people were killed by arsonists, who burnt their apartment block to the ground.

This was at a low-income tenement building on Orange Lane in Kingston's inner-city.

So brutal were the terrorists who set the fire in the dead of night, that they prevented those who got awake and tried to escape from the inferno from doing so, by wildly firing shots at them.

Even babies were not spared, as it was reported that some gunmen even grabbed infants from their rescuers *and threw them back* into the burning building.

This was probably the most sickening and horrific crime ever committed in the country as it involved the deliberate burning to death of helpless children.

After each act of terrorism, both parties sought to try to influence public opinion by blaming the other side for every monstrous act.

However, I sincerely believe some of the dastardliest acts were carried out by the government and its party activists, to try to cast blame on the opposition and justify the state of emergency.

One of the claims the government liked to make too, was that the *American CIA* was active in Jamaica assisting the JLP to destabilize the PNP government because of its closeness to Castro, so they planned the most vicious atrocities.

According to them therefore, the horrible acts of violence occurring, were being carried out by the CIA to shock the nation into blaming the government!

A year after the Orange Lane Fire, a commission of enquiry was held into that monstrous event, under the chairmanship of a highly respected former Supreme Court Judge Ronald Small, a man whose family had always been politically involved with the ruling PNP.

Among his published findings was the confirmation that Manley's minister of housing, Anthony Spaulding, who had always been rumored to be involved in arming gunmen and directing affairs in his garrison constituency located at Arnett Gardens which is close to Orange Lane; *"...was a man with more than a blushing acquaintance with gunmen."*

The full report of the Commission of Enquiry into the Orange Lane fire *is well hidden* in the Rare Books section of the library at Institute of Jamaica at East Street in Kingston).

However, the clearly fearful Commissioner Small would not go as far as attributing responsibility, so he never said or even implied who had been *directly* responsible for that dastardly act in the dangerously polarized country of ours.

Subsequent leaks by a close family member years later, revealed that Small's entire family had to live with serious threats to their lives during the period when that enquiry was being conducted by him.

Although I must divert a bit, I personally experienced Minister Spaulding's "blushing acquaintance with gunmen" which Small referred to above.

At that time, the Cubans seemed to be virtually in charge of our country to the point where, at a party I attended a few nights before at the home of a senior official of the JLP, the Cuban Ambassador Ulysses Estrada, who was also rumored to be the head of the Cuban DGI and lived nearby, unceremoniously invaded Henry's private premises and threatened the host with *physical violence* if he did not turn down the music!

It was shortly after that event, that *Estrada*, went on the government owned national television and threatened *"....to bring in his soldiers to deal with those of us who were criticizing his government."*

Some of us were so incensed by this brazen threat by him in our own country, that the JLP drafted a letter to the prime minister, demanding that Estrada be immediately *expelled* from Jamaica. To deliver the letter, quite a few hundred of us marched with the courier, to the prime minister's office at Jamaica House on Hope Road in Kingston.

However, the soldiers at the gate would not allow us to enter the property or even accept the letter.

While we were arguing with them, up drove a car in which we saw the same minister, *Anthony Spaulding* sitting in the back. Beside him was a man whom I did not recognize but immediately saw as he raised a gun through the back window and aimed those of us who were at the front of the crowd.

I later learnt that the shooter had been one of the most brutal political assassins from Spaulding's constituency, a man called *"Red Tony"* or *"Tony Red,"* I really do not recall exactly.

What I do remember however is that I broke every record that *Usain Bolt* could only dream of. As on seeing the gun aimed at us, I ran non-stop from Hope Road to Belmont Road, where the JLP headquarters is located, around five miles.

I was clearly only propelled by adrenalin, for I never even knew that I was running barefooted, until I reached my destination and someone asked me what had happened to my shoes.

I had absolutely no idea where they fell off my feet as I fled in panic!

At the time, the police force had been totally politicized with most senior officers openly working along with Manley's political agenda. So, when we reported the attack on us by a known criminal, an Inspector of police did visit the JLP headquarters and took statements from all who saw the shooter, but that was only to impress the independent media, as the matter died there.

The Green Bay Massacre

The Green Bay Massacre was executed by soldiers in the Jamaica Defense Force, (JDF) our official army, on January 5, 1978, to assist Prime Minister Michael Manley keep better control in his constituency.

I have no doubt that Manley himself *initiated* the entire sordid affair, since the army fell directly under his portfolio and the men killed, were his open and vocal *detractors.*

In Manley's constituency, there was a small JLP enclave called *Southside* where unemployed opposition supporters were demanding that jobs being given out by the government, be distributed *equally* between JLP and PNP supporters.

This simple demand *for justice and fairness* was regarded as, them not only defying Manley's authority but also making pests of themselves.

The Military Intelligence Unit (MIU), the undercover division of the army, was therefore mandated to single out the *troublesome* fellows, and trick them into believing that they would be transported to the army's target range at Green Bay in St. Catherine where they also operated a small port. The young men were promised that they would be employed there to load a ship.

As pre-arranged, they were picked up by an ambulance belonging to the army. When they arrived at Green Bay, they were instructed to walk ahead of the soldiers but as they reached the pre-determined point, *an army sniper hiding in the bushes opened fire on them.*

Five of the seven young men taken there were killed on the spot, but fortunately two were able to escape, though seriously injured.

The initial information disseminated by the army, had been that; "they had surprised some men unloading guns from a boat, the men fired at them, the army returned fire and the men were killed."

It was only because one of the two who escaped, was able to get to and elicit the assistance of *Sister Benedict Chung*, a Roman Catholic nun who was doing charitable work in their section of the inner-city, that the true story was leaked to investigative journalists at the Gleaner newspaper and eventually publicized.

One investigative journalist, David DaCosta, somehow obtained a roll of film from a camera owned by one of the officers involved in the operation.

On that film were pictures of the officer's family at the beach, but fortunately for Jamaica, the film also recorded some shots from a part of the exercise at Green Bay. It was from how the shadows were cast at the time of the assault, that DaCosta was able to find experts who were able to discount the Army's timeline and *substantiate fully*, the survivor's version.

A *show trial* followed, but the perpetrators got off scot free as the entire thing had been initiated from on high.

The Manley family was the closest thing we had to *royalty* in Jamaica. Also, the tall, handsome, charismatic Michael Manley who was a demagogue, was adept at manipulating people and especially women, so had no difficulty becoming a "Teflon" politician in the eyes of many, regardless of the evidence proving that he was *personally* behind many of the bloodiest events of the period.

The line the non-believers and his *propogandists* has always used, was that none of the bloody massacres, including the Green Bay Massacre, were initiated on Manley's orders but instead by the *leftists,* who had seized control of the party.

Absolute baloney!

Nothing could be further from the truth for regardless of what appeared to be happening, as a former activist in that party, I know as a fact that Manley *always* retained *full control* of his party.

Gold Street Massacre

The mass slaughter which I know most about was the Gold Street Massacre which took place in April 1980. This was when heavily armed gunmen traveled in canoes from the open sea and fired on a

dance in progress at Gold Street, in downtown
Kingston, killing several people.

*Once again this was in Prime Minister Michael
Manley's constituency.*

Because of the precision with which that assault
had been carried out, killing five persons and
injuring more than a dozen, I had always assumed
that the Cubans who were visible all over Jamaica
at the time, had led that mission.

Years later, I learnt *quite by accident*, that it was
done by our own home-grown terrorists, some of
whom had been trained as "brigadistas" in Cuba.

The first time I ever visited Gold Street, which was
also a JLP enclave in Manley's constituency,
coincidentally the very same area from which the
army had lured the seven young men who they
ambushed at Green Bay, was shortly after the Star,
an evening tabloid, carried a story reporting how
JLP supporters had staged a "mock funeral" for
Michael Manley and his wife Beverly.

Events such as these were quite common on the
Jamaican political scene, where for decades,
supporters all political parties, have relished
building elaborate coffins, to *playfully bury,*
various persons from the opposing party, to show
that they are *politically dead.*

There had never been any violent intentions or reactions, when these mock funerals were staged in the past, as they were just considered an age-old method of political dissention, performed in good fun.

When the story was published, I had been volunteering almost full time at the JLP headquarters in their public relations (PR) department.

This was in the olden days when video cameras were not widely known or used. In fact, the only one *I had seen up to then,* was the huge one carried by the cameramen at the local television station.

Also volunteering with me in the PR department, was a wealthy Englishman by the name of Phil Harvey who had lived in Jamaica for years.

He was a close member of the well-respected family that owned and produced the internationally known brand, Harvey's Bristol Cream Sherry and he later became one of the founders of the Jamaican Film Industry.

Phil said he owned a video camera and when he saw the story in the newspaper with pictures of the attractively decorated coffin at the mock funeral, he suggested to me that we go downtown and videotape the procession for possible propaganda purposes later.

So off we went to Gold Street, having contacted someone there who had promised to have the scene we saw in the newspaper, re-enacted. It was quite a jolly affair with everyone *being a film star for a day* and we the directors. The large group of residents who came out, enjoyed themselves immensely as they walked somberly with the flower-decorated coffin on their heads, in which lay the effigies of Manley and his wife, as directed.

They even sang funeral hymns as they ambled along.

Little did we know or expect that retaliation to what was just innocent fun, would have been a *swift, bloody assault on revelers,* the very next night as they attended a fund-raising dance.

But in retrospect, maybe we should have known that "dissing" (disrespecting) the ultimate leader, *not once but twice,* would have really angered him and his supporters.

I have always felt a measure of guilt for possibly contributing to that retaliation therefore. For if the mock funeral had not been re-enacted, maybe, *just maybe,* the bloodthirsty, vengeful, power hungry ones would not have attacked the innocent revelers.

An update; as I stated earlier, I had always thought that raid had been carried out by the Cubans or even under their supervision. For in my book it had been too precise to have been implemented by our usually, unsophisticated gangsters. Besides, the terrorists had come in from the sea to launch the attack and I had *never* heard of anything like that happening in Jamaica before.

I was only disabused of that impression, many years later.

This happened sometime in the mid-1980's, after I had become quite friendly with a former president of the PNP Youth Organization (PNPYO), Norris MacDonald.

We had both been doing political commentaries at the now defunct JBC (Jamaica Broadcasting Corporation) for airing on their radio station, after the change of government in 1980. Then, all political views were being welcomed by the station as they tried to restore their damaged credibility.

For during the 70's that government-owned media organization, had been nothing but an extension of the PNP party. (As Fox news is for the Republican party in the USA.) So, the news was nothing but party-political propaganda.

As the station's reputation had been totally shattered, it had to be quickly restored. With the change of government therefore, views from various sectors were being facilitated.

Norris had suggested to me that since we had both been political activists on *opposite sides* and knew the inner workings of the parties, we should do a political investigative/discussion program for television.

As we explored various formats to determine the types of interviews we would conduct, one of the places we visited was a section of Manley's stronghold at Hanover Street in downtown Kingston. There Norris introduced me to a young man whose first name I cannot recall, but his surname was Mothersill, a most uncommon name in Jamaica.

He claimed to be the area leader, so during a wide and varied conversation, I started slipping in questions to him about the *Gold Street massacre,* since it had been carried out in that very constituency.

I confided to him how I thought it had been carried out by the Cubans; *a)* because of the precision of the attack and *b*) the fact that the attackers had come from the sea, something unprecedented in Jamaica.

His answer was immediate, boastful and terse; "*No a wi dweet!*" (No, we did it!)

When he realized what he had inadvertently revealed, he refused to continue with any more information except to admit that the police had detained and questioned him about it at the time, but because they had no evidence to hold him or anyone else, no one was arrested.

I had to cease asking anything further about the massacre, as the rapid change in his attitude made me realize that I was treading in dangerous waters!

AN ACT OF TREASON

The implications of what became dubbed as the *Moonex Affair* were the most far-reaching for Jamaica as a sovereign nation and even raised the real possibility that our then minister of security, Dudley Thompson, had been involved in *treason*.

On the 7th May, 1980, an innocent looking cargo on a boat arriving in Jamaica was being randomly inspected by Customs officers when to their shock, they discovered that the shipment included 19,000 pounds of ammunition totaling *200,000 bullets* for shotguns.

The goods were consigned to a firm in Kingston named Moonex International, the manager of which was one Ruperto Hart.

It was soon revealed in the only independent newspaper operating at the time, the Daily Gleaner, that Moonex was a Cuban-owned company and it was *they* who were attempting to smuggle in the bullets under diplomatic cover.

At first, the serving Cuban Ambassador and apparent DGI boss, Ulysses Estrada, vehemently denied that Moonex had anything to do with Cuba. He quickly got the willing assistance of persons in the government-owned JBC newsroom, as he tried to do damage control.

At that time, the publicly owned JBC radio and television stations, were staffed only by persons who spouted Democratic Socialism. They were therefore totally loyal to the government and carried *only* news that was beneficial to the ruling party, even when they had to manufacture it.

However, an article in the Venezuelan magazine **Zeta** in June 1980, revealed that;

"Moonex is one of the many companies which is used by Castro's people to introduce their agents and spies into other countries. All of them, like Moonex, are in the absolute ownership of the Cuban dictatorship and their executives are selected by the Intelligence Service."

The full extent of our own Security Minister's treachery and his attempt to cover up on behalf of the Cubans, further unfolded in an investigative report in the Gleaner dated June 19, 1980 entitled; "Moonex man barred from flying to Cuba, was in a plane with Thompson, Estrada."

The article stated in part;

"Moonex International establishment manager Ruperto Hart was yesterday prevented by Immigration officials at the Norman Manley

Airport (in Jamaica) from going on a flight to Cuba on which other passengers were National Security Minister Dudley Thompson and Cuban Ambassador Ulises Estrada. Hart, whose company had illegally imported shotgun cartridges which had arrived here from Miami in a consignment without an import license, is on an Immigration Department's 'Watch List.' A 'stop order' preventing him from travelling out of the island is in force. Minister Thompson made the trip alone, as Mr. Estrada elected to remain behind with Mr. Hart after the Immigration authorities prevented Mr. Hart from leaving. Reports reaching the GLEANER are that yesterday afternoon the travel documents of Thompson, Estrada and Hart were processed by Immigration at Norman Manley International airport for a flight to Cuba. Their baggage was loaded on a Cubana flight; but they boarded a smaller plane. By this time Immigration officials found that Hart was on their "Watch List" and went to the small aircraft which they learned he had boarded. Mr. Hart had been warned for prosecution under two sections of the Customs Act in connection with a consignment of shotgun cartridges which arrived at Bustamante Port on May 5. The GLEANER understands that further legal action was to be taken against him this week. On the plane when the Immigration officials boarded it, the Gleaner understands, was Minister

Thompson sitting at the back with his face covered by a paper. Immigration authorities said they were told that Hart was "A Ministry official."

A Ministry official! Can you believe the level of treachery that the *Minister of Security* of Jamaica was involved in, with the full consent of Manley himself, I have no doubt!

So serious had been the implications of the Moonex affair however, that even the powerful, often-compliant Jamaica Council of Churches, (JCC) had to speak out against Minister Thompson. I say *even* as that umbrella organization which represented most of the churches at that time, had been captured by so-called "liberation theologists." They had actively promoted the socialist philosophy to the point where they were even branded by the opposition as *the PNP at prayer!*

However, even they did not seem prepared to *condone treason*, for they joined many other respected organizations which put out a statement in the press, calling on prime minister Manley to revoke Dudley Thompson's appointment as Minister of Security, and he did.

SAVED BY PATRIOTS

Of course, some persons may be wondering how so many people in the *system*, were, in such dangerous times, not only leaking so much information about what was happening but also enforcing the law against powerful government officials.

Thankfully, there were numerous patriotic Jamaicans working all over in the government service, (like your whistleblower in the USA!) who had previously supported Manley, but on seeing what was happening, decided that they did not want Cuba to *take over* our country.

It was obvious therefore that they made the decision, *death before dishonor*, for they took many risks to leak information about dangerous practices within the government, to help to save the country and its citizens from losing their freedoms.

The leaking of sensitive information to the media and the JLP on a regular basis, therefore became quite critical, for it further mobilized the public against the direction in which the government was leading the country.

It also enabled the opposition to gain credibility with international organizations such as Amnesty

International and the International Press Association (IAPA.)

Fortunately for us also, while Manley was attracted to the grandeur of the type of supreme power that Castro enjoyed in Cuba, he also wanted to be regarded as a *democrat,* and a leader for the Third World countries, by the outside world, when he attended international events at the United Nations and the Non-Aligned Conference.

So, he was constantly trying to do a balancing act, pulling back whenever his government was caught going too far.

As the independent media in the USA were also keeping an eagle eye on developments in their backyard, they gave the opposition, wide coverage, thus preventing Manley from taking too many more retaliatory, oppressive and overt actions against those fighting to preserve democracy.

Further, Manley loved being adored and idolized locally so when he started to sense the mounting dislike and loss of personal and party support because of the unpopular and often damaging socialist policies, *he waffled regularly*, even frequently giving in to the JLP's militant demands that enquiries be held into the various atrocities like the Green Bay and Gold Street massacres.

The enquiries held were however all for show, simply to appease vocal critics and overseas donors.

No one was therefore ever brought to justice for any of the acts of treason or terrorism committed against innocent civilians by the army and the police.

By the latter part of 1980, not even everyone in Manley's cabinet was prepared to sell-out Jamaica's interest to the Cubans, for senior Ministers David Coore, Eric Bell and Vivian Blake all resigned from the cabinet although they said *nothing* to the Jamaican people about why they were leaving.

However, a junior minister named Allan Isaacs not only resigned but crossed the floor and joined the JLP in the fight to turn back his former colleagues, who were destroying the economy with their socialist policies while appearing to be dead set on making Jamaica the second USSR satellite in the Caribbean.

He contested the election for the JLP in St. Andrew South Eastern in December 1980 and won the seat.

As I relate this, I must insist that not only Jamaicans from my generation but also from generations to come, owe *an eternal debt of gratitude* to whomever it was that leaked the information about that shipment of 200,000 bullets. For if the existence of the contents of that shipment had not been revealed, thousands of Jamaicans would have been massacred and our fate would have been totally different.

As the undeclared civil war raged on at the local level, almost every constituency in Jamaica saw some form of violence being perpetuated by either the JLP, the PNP or the USSR-sponsored, Workers Party of Jamaica, (WPJ) led by a University of the West Indies professor, Dr Trevor Munroe who supported the PNP.

By the end of 1980, the number of murders in the tiny island with a population of just over two and half million residents, had quadrupled, for the combatants were well armed.

In fact, I can't recall going to bed any night without hearing in the background, the sound of numerous gunshots.

So, travelling around, one had to know which areas to avoid, for in some zones, just being an outsider could lead to your death.

It was mainly underprivileged young men who were killed or injured however, as they were the foot soldiers and therefore in the line on fire.

However, a few months prior to the 1980 election, a former JLP Prime Minister, Hugh Lawson Shearer, was shot in his head *with a spear gun* by PNP terrorists as he travelled, through the north coast town of Falmouth in the parish of Trelawny.

He survived.

The only high-level politician who was killed during that period, was a parliamentary secretary in the Ministry of Security, named Roy McGann.

He was slain in a shootout with police the night before Nomination Day for the 1980 election.

Naturally the politically aligned police would never have *knowingly* fired on a group including a government parliamentarian, but they never knew he was there.

They had received a report that gunmen from opposing parties were trading shots in the Gordon Town area of rural St. Andrew.

According to the news, the police confronted the first group of the miscreants they saw and when the smoke had cleared, it was discovered that

McGann himself and his police bodyguard had been killed.

That led to a series of reprisals against JLP supporters in the Gordon Town area. Many were beaten, others burnt out of their homes and otherwise terrorized for days as the *politically-aligned* members of the police force, invaded the area with blood in their eyes and revenge in their hearts.

Most of my activities leading up to the 1980 elections, were as a member of the Nationalist Patriotic Movement (NPM). This was a youth group established under the mentorship of Pernell Charles, a veteran JLP politician and deputy leader.

We the members of this youth movement, *were young, unafraid, loved street politics* like painting graffiti, and *would demonstrate at the drop of a pin.*

Our most successful demonstration was the memorable Gas Demonstration of 1979 which caused the entire country to be locked down by roadblocks for three full days.

Incidentally it was the former prime minister, Michael Manley himself, who first taught

Jamaicans how to block roads. He used that method most effectively, in a strike some years before, at Jamaica Broadcasting Corporation (JBC), the government-owned radio and television company, when he was a labor leader in search of political fame.

The 1979 gas demonstration had the most long-lasting effect on me personally though, as it led to me being detained at Cross Roads police station and facing a possible mandatory prison term of *indefinite detention* for having, shell casings from M16 rifles.

I say long lasting effect, for when I was locked up, I was given a cigarette to calm my nerves and that led me to take back up and continue with a vice I had discarded many years before!

The *mandatory indefinite detention* sentence referred to above was legislated in 1974, when two friends of Prime Minister Manley were shot and killed in close succession. That caused him to establish an institution called the "Gun Court" where, under the accompanying legislation, anyone found with even *one* spent shell, would face a sentence of mandatory, indefinite detention.

I was detained because I had a handful of shell casings.

I had them, because I was at the JLP headquarters one day when we got word that some peaceful demonstrators who were marching from downtown Kingston to the headquarters, had been *fired on* by police and soldiers. We decided to march to the spot where we heard the assault had taken place, to assist the injured and show solidarity to their cause.

On arriving near Cross Roads, which is halfway between uptown and downtown Kingston, we met upon a small group of people, looking battered and scared. They were walking slowly and had been in the demonstration but had not run away or been seriously injured when the barrage of shots had been fired into the crowd by the police.

They took us to a spot not too far away and pointed to several spent M16 automatic rifle shells lying on the ground. These were the casings left behind when the police fired into the group that was demonstrating, they told us.

I immediately collected a handful of the spent shells with the intention of presenting them to the appropriate authorities, as evidence of *police brutality* against peaceful demonstrators.

As we walked towards the nearest police station, led by senior members of the party, I felt something hard and cold being thrust in my back.

When I turned around, I realized that it was a long machine gun being held by a soldier who shouted that he was going to have me locked up for having *dangerous weapons*. (ie. The spent shells.)

I was scared out of my wits, for to begin with, I am terribly claustrophobic, so the possibility of being locked up in small, hot, dirty cell, was immediately terrifying. Worse, as I walked along in front of him, I had visions of him tripping and the gun going off and blowing a big hole in my back.

Anyway, even if I didn't get killed, there was still the specter of my being locked up indefinitely in a nasty Jamaican jail. For the stinking conditions under which prisoners were being held, were no secret.

In fact, this had even attracted much condemnation from Amnesty International, for which I had sometimes been a local correspondent.

I was taken to the police station at Cross Roads and told to sit on a bench with other prisoners who were waiting to be processed.

I was a nervous wreck as I was kept waiting for about four hours without any attempt being made to lay charges against me or even being allowed to make a phone call.

Every time I enquired about my fate, I was told that the arresting officer was not around so I would just have to sit there and keep myself quiet.

I sat quietly for another few hours, getting hungrier by the minute, then saw a policeman who I knew.

When he enquired what I was doing there, I told him of the trumped-up charges and complained that I was hungry, wanted my lunch or even some water as the place was hot and crowded. He told me that lunch had already been served but as I was not yet officially in custody, I was not entitled to have any food anyway.

He assured me that I would not like prisoners' lunch however as it was only *boiled rice*. It sounded *yucky* but I told him that the way my tummy was feeling, I would gladly have downed even *tasteless* boiled rice.

He left and about half an hour later, returned with a small brown paper bag and gave me a cold Guinness stout and a cigarette which he said he had bought with his own funds. I thanked him profusely and although I did not like stout and had stopped smoking a few years before, that ale tasted wonderful as did the cigarette.

Hence my taking up the smoking vice again.

The police were at that time, a law unto themselves, having been given supreme power under the State of Emergency. So, I feared that I would be in jail for a long while, although not charged.

Neither was there any mention of how or when I would get bail.

I guess in my desperation I must have fallen asleep, since I am notorious for sleeping anywhere any time. I really don't know how much time elapsed before I was awakened by a boisterous commotion outside the holding area, caused by a loud booming voice asking *for me* by name.

That most welcome voice was that of a well-known Queens Council (QC) Winston Spaulding who was then a deputy leader of the JLP but after the 1980 election, became the Minister of Security.

Spaulding was also the younger brother of Anthony Spaulding the PNP minister who had become so notorious that he had been described as; 'a man with more than a *passing acquaintance with gunmen*' in the report done after the enquiry into the Orange lane fire.

Winston too had been a PNP member but in an interview with the Jamaica Observer in 2002, he candidly declared; "I grew up in a PNP household but after the State of Emergency, and the passing of 1974 Gun Court law, I had a problem with the significant human rights abuses of the time. It was a question of conscience."

Spaulding loudly upbraided the officer in charge for detaining me *illegally* as I had only been gathering evidence of police brutality. He warned them that he had lots of witnesses to testify that this was so and he was going to report the matter to every Human Rights body in the world.

It took him only about fifteen minutes to get me out of there.

I remain eternally grateful to him for that, for the couple hours I had spent without my freedom of movement made me appreciate even more, how important *my liberty* is to me.

Apart from getting involved in demonstrations and other forms of street activity, we the NPM members, were prepared to confront the PNP/WPJ/Cubans on any matter.

On one occasion when our parent party (the JLP) refused to participate in debates which were being organized by another government propaganda arm, the Jamaica Information Service, (JIS), we decided that we would take them on.

The JLP's boycott of those events was justified anyway, as these fora being staged island-wide, were not really being held to disseminate information to the public, but simply to shore up the PNP's propaganda machinery. For the practice was to use taxpayer's money to transport large number of socialist-supporters to the venues to *harass* and *intimidate* opposition participants.

Further, the panels were terribly skewed with the JIS, PNP and WPJ, reciting the same lines and shouting down the sole opposition spokesperson whenever he or she spoke.

I clearly remember the debate I volunteered to participate in, on behalf of the NPM.

This was a discussion on the economy which was rapidly slipping into the doldrums and driving citizens to the edge of penury at the time, due to Manley's socialist policies.

The forum was being held in the Garveymeade Community Centre in Portmore in the parish of St. Catherine.

Knowing from my days as a PNP activist, how they operated at functions such as these, I went to a nearby JLP stronghold called Naggo Head, also in St. Catherine, to recruit party supporters to come out to cheer for me at the debate. I told them up front that only very vocal persons should come! I even paid out of my own pocket, for two buses to transport them to the venue.

My straightforward instructions to them were; "Cheer loudly whenever I speak and boo and hiss loudly when PNP, JIS or WPJ representatives open their mouths!"

In addition, I had several packages containing pamphlets criticizing the government's economic policies. I gave those to my supporters when they boarded the buses, instructing that they should hand them out to everyone at the venue, as soon as they arrived.

On arrival, I went inside to where the panel had already assembled.

Everyone had been vociferous, confident and eager as we travelled to the event, but shortly after I sat down, I heard loud noises and shouting coming from outside.

We all ran out to find out what caused the disturbance, only to see all *my* supporters scrambling wildly to get into the buses which were already revving loudly. When the drivers figured everyone had boarded, they took off at top speed into the night with a loud roar.

I subsequently learnt that as my supporters gave out the pamphlets, a well-known vicious PNP assassin nicknamed *Early Bird,* from the violent Matthews Lane stronghold in Kingston, had immediately grabbed one and on seeing what it said, snarled and used his lighter to set it on fire, right in front of my supporters.

He then demanded that all other persons with pamphlets bring them and throw them down at his feet, *or else.*

I had never heard of Early Bird before but some of my supporters knew of his reputation as a vicious killer.

So, there I was, abandoned by my *cheering team* and left totally alone to face a hostile audience.

However, I was too proud and stubborn to slink off into the night, although that is what my better instincts were telling me to do.

So, I decided to return to the hall and make the best of a bad situation.

Luckily for me, a very tall, strong young man named Magnus Williams, who was a JLP supporter had remained behind, but I did not know that until later.

He was a friend who lived beside our farm in Spanish Town. He was a courageous political activist who was at the time the Councilor caretaker for the Duncan's Pen division. He had not travelled in the bus to the debate with my paid cheering crowd but had driven over by himself.

When he saw my dilemma, he came up to the platform and insisted that I should not participate in the debate. I was overjoyed to see him but resisted, telling him that I would *not* be intimidated by a bunch of loud, menacing socialists.

When the debate began however it was a different ballgame, for every-time I tried to make a point, my words were immediately drowned out by loud boos and hisses coming from the audience.

I don't think I completed one entire sentence that night for they were using the very same strategy I had hoped to use on them when, I had collected the two busloads of supporters.

My paid cheering crowd had however abandoned me and it had come back to haunt me!

Then I saw Magnus once again approaching the platform. Without saying a word, he picked me up, threw me over his shoulder and carried me out of the room to the sound of loud *boos and hisses.*

I don't know if that night I was more frightened by the fearsome sight of the assassin, Early Bird, or the taunts of the loud hostile crowd, but I tried to put on a brave face.

That experience clearly demonstrated to us in the NPM, why the senior politicians in the JLP had been avoiding those debates organized by the JIS.

After that night, we too boycotted *every event* organized by government agencies.

Another role I undertook in the party was as a caretaker in a Constituency Division at Naggo Head in St. Catherine.

In this position, I had a responsibility to organize at the grassroots level, by visiting many homes, canvassing the votes, sending workers to convince their neighbors to get registered to vote etc.

My long-term plan was to work towards getting elected as the Councilor to represent that zone in the St. Catherine Parish Council.

This was in a deep rural area where the people were mainly struggling tradesmen and farmers. However, although the civil war was raging in streets of the towns, it was reasonably calm and safe there.

Despite not having any political violence in the vicinity, on several visits I would be approached by young man, asking me how they could get guns.

On pointing out that there was no need for guns and telling them I had none, they would insist that there were plenty at the JLP headquarters, so I should acquire some for that division as their political opponents were being armed.

I was however never interested in getting involved in that aspect of politics and truthfully, although I was at the headquarters almost every day for about two years, I never heard of a strong room, an arm's room or any such section there.

Neither did I ever ask anyone if I could get arms or from where.

Anyway, they kept insisting that they should be armed as one could never tell when they needed to defend themselves.

Soon however, I was shocked into reality.

I had to visit the area to meet with some senior organizers in the division.

Where that meeting was being held, was in an even more remote and depressed area than usual, so I had to park my car and walk a few hundred yards to the venue. There were no street lights there so it was quite dark.

After the meeting, an old man *who reeked of stale rum,* approached me and told me that as it was dark and possibly dangerous, I should not be walking back to the car by myself.

He then took it on himself to accompany me, *to protect* me, he said.

He looked so old, shaky and clearly drunk that I decided to humor him by not objecting.

When I arrived back at the car, I opened the door and the light came on. That is when I realized that he was holding a gun in his hand!

All I could think of on the way home, was how lucky I had been that he had not stumbled in his drunken state and accidentally shot me!

The point is, in the months leading up to the 1980 elections, just about everyone involved in politics on *all* sides, seemed to have access to guns if they wished and many were certainly using them.

In fact, I clearly recall one day driving from the party headquarters to the JBC radio station to deliver a news release, as in those days, there were no smart phones or emails, so hard copies of news releases had to be taken in to the media houses manually.

As I waited at a busy intersection for the traffic light to change to green, I heard a bullet *zing* past my right ear.

I had no idea where it came from but I never stopped at a traffic light again for that entire day!

I vividly remember too, the graphic reports of the incident that took place on the *nomination day* for the 1980 general election.

This was in the St. Andrew South constituency which was represented by Ms. Portia Simpson-Miller, who later became *Jamaica's first female Prime Minister*.

This constituency was known to be especially dangerous, and in fact considered a "garrison" of the ruling party.

Garrisons were heavily armed areas controlled by the political parties in Jamaica. There, you find a concentration of gunmen, many of whom were trained and ready to be deployed to other parts of the country as the necessity arose.

On the fateful nomination day, the JLP's candidate, Tavares-Finson, had to be transported to the nomination center in *an army tank*. This was because, each time he and his supporters tried to drive in a section of Spanish Town Road, a main thoroughfare running from Kingston to western Jamaica, they were forced to turn back because they came under heavy gunfire.

As bad as things were, I had never heard of another incident anywhere else in the entire island where a candidate had to be escorted by an army tank to a nomination center.

I suspect however that the army was only brought in to protect the *opposition candidate*, because by then, the country was swarming with members of the foreign press and lots of international election observers, including many deployed by the United Nations.

These foreigners were being accommodated, as the late prime minister Michael Manley saw himself as a leader of the "third world," so tried to cultivate a positive image as a democrat, to burnish his *international* reputation.

He therefore tried to do everything, including allowing in foreign observer missions for those elections, to try and convince the outside world that he was not really just an undemocratic despot, schooled by Cuban handlers, despite the evidence to the contrary.

During the entire 1980, therefore, the undeclared, mini civil-war raged everywhere in Jamaica to different degrees, but it was especially fierce in the ghettos in Kingston and Spanish Town.

Not even school children were spared because if they were seen wearing the *wrong color* school uniform, they became instant targets! For in those days, the official color of the JLP was *green* and the PNP *orange* while the miniscule USSR-sponsored communist party, the WPJ, used red.

While neither the poor kids nor their parents had much control over the color of the uniform their school used, nor could they attend school without being neatly clad in the appropriate garb, no one had ever dreamt that a day would come in Jamaica when the color of a school uniform could be considered politically offensive and endanger the lives of children!

But it did, so kids who had to pass through, or lived in hostile areas solidly loyal to one party or the other, could not wear the *wrong* colors!

If they were unfortunate enough to be mandated to wear a color uniform that was not in sync with the color of the dominant party in the area, they were often ordered to take off the displeasing color; their parents had to send them to school in ordinary non-offending clothes or simply keep them home.

During that period therefore, children in the ghettos, lost hundreds of valuable school hours because of violence or threats.

Of course, children of the political elite were not affected as they certainly did not live in the worse affected areas.

While this dangerous intimidation of students wearing the *wrong* colors was pervasive in the poorer sections of the capital city, Montego Bay and Spanish Town, I was absolutely amazed when it was reported in a newscast one day, that the administration of a school in the mid-island town of Mandeville, had closed that institution for more than a week because of the threats to the lives of its students wearing their *green* uniforms.

This was an especially distressing report, as it was coming out of what was always considered a reasonably peaceful rural community.

The point is, so dangerous and polarized had our small island become, that had this action been taken by a school administrator in *the urban area,* it would not even have made the news!

While the violence continued unabated in the streets, Manley tried to stifle our democracy even more by taking aim at press freedom, something we held most sacred.

Yes, the government owned and controlled our only television station, one of the two radio stations and one of the two daily newspapers. However, their media enjoyed little credibility with free-thinking people, who instead turned to the independently run radio station, Radio Jamaica and Reddifusion (RJR), and the privately-owned daily newspaper, the Gleaner, for the truth.

As the Gleaner was the most influential medium in the country because it had a solid cadre of fearless columnists and editorial writers, one day the government mandated that the newspaper should send its investigative articles and columns to parliament for approval, *before publication!*

It was only the courage of the outstanding staff there who refused to comply, despite numerous threats to their lives, liberty and property, *why we still have the press freedom we continue to enjoy in Jamaica today.*

When the newspaper started to run low on funds because the government and its lackeys in the business sector, withdrew advertising support from the publication, the management issued a debenture and the Jamaican public put their money where their mouths were and over-subscribed to it.

Then the government attempted to restrict the importation of newsprint for the newspaper, claiming that this was done as we had a chronic shortage of foreign exchange, so they had to allocate funds to those importing food, not newsprint.

This strategy had been implemented in Guyana, which was led at the time by Manley's fellow socialist *anti-press-freedom* colleague, the late prime minister Forbes Burnham.

He had succeeded in crippling the independent newspapers there which were critical of his regime, by cutting off their newsprint supplies.

However, Manley's attempt to crush our press freedom in Jamaica was frustrated, due to the majority of the people being fully mobilized by the militant opposition, who told us up front what the government was really up to.

So, the government's announcement about restricting foreign exchange to import newsprint was immediately met with strong condemnation from most sectors in the society, overseas allies and massive demonstrations in the streets.

Manley could have sent his brigadistas and the security forces into the streets to quell the demonstrations as they sometimes did, and gone ahead with restricting the importation of newsprint, but as I said before, with all the foreign press swarming the country in the months leading up to the elections, he wanted to keep up the pretense of being a democrat and favoring press freedom.

In frustration at seeing how firmly the Jamaican public stood for freedom of the press, Manley, accompanied by the Cuban ambassador Ulysses Estrada, could only pathetically lead a march of his rowdy, threatening socialist activists and supporters, to the Gleaner newspaper's offices downtown, to verbally intimidate the reporters and columnists.

Angrily they shouted threats of *"next time."* meaning no doubt that the next time, the staff would not get off so easy!

It was a grateful Oliver Clarke, former chairman and managing director of the Gleaner who in 2000, at that newspaper's 165th anniversary celebration, reminded the nation about the company's struggle to survive. In an emotional address he said in part;

"In the middle 1970's, the Gleaner was a major advocate of private enterprise and democracy in Jamaica. As a result, it came into sharp conflict with the Michael Manley-led government of the time. The company was in bad financial condition. The stock market was in the doldrums. So, we put out a debenture issue for the grand sum of four million Jamaican dollars. At the time it was the biggest public offering in the history of Jamaica. People rallied around; it was oversubscribed. Even more than the money was the strong vote of confidence demonstrated by the public for the Gleaner. Many major businesses supported the debenture, as well as many hundreds of individuals. This success allowed The Gleaner to pay off its major debts and widen its shareholder base. The debenture issue gave the company a whole new breath of life."

In retrospect, one major factor that helped to save us in Jamaica from *socialism,* during that cold war era was *Manley's pride.*

For if we did not have a prime minister who valued his image abroad and wanted to be regaled as a democrat in international fora, the commissions of enquires into the various massacres and even the general election in the 1980, may never have been held, despite the support the opposition party was getting from democratic governments all over the world.

For look at how **Madura** is continuing to oppress the people, curb press freedom and hold on to power in Venezuela, despite international pressure and the turmoil at home!

He clearly does not care how he is regarded abroad.

However, despite pulling back on the measures to restrict press freedom generally, individual journalists who were not towing the government's line, were constantly under threat of physical harm. One Gleaner columnist, John Hearne, who had been a PNP supporter for decades and Michael Manley's *best friend*, was beaten to within an inch of his life, when he attended the next PNP party conference, something he had always participated in for most of his adult life.

This was because when Hearne, saw the brutality of the government he once supported was wreaking against those in opposition, and the destructive socialist policies they were inflicting on the nation, he had started to criticize them in his columns.

MY FORAY INTO JOURNALISM

Because of a love of writing which I developed in high school, I had added the use of the press to my cache of ammunition, in fighting against the attempt to introduce socialism into my country.

At first, I launched a massive personal letter writing campaign against just about everything the government did. My letters were regularly being published in the Gleaner and finally caught the attention of the editor, who offered me a weekly column in the newspaper, *with pay and all.*

At that time, it was popular to write under a nom de plume and I deliberately chose as mine, *Kathrine G. Burgess,* as when shortened, it became KGB.

This is because at that time, all who opposed the government were accused of being paid by the American CIA, so I thought it appropriate and hilarious even, to be writing *anti-socialist articles* under "KGB!"

Another weapon I chose to use to fight the socialist regime in my own country and influence the electorate as much as I could, was participating in the nightly call-in program aired on radio.

At the time, there was only one such program, and it was aired on the government-owned radio, JBC. The host was of course a ranking PNP member, Ronnie Thwaites, who became a minister of education when the PNP was returned to power, in 1989 after *disavowing socialism*!

Naturally, he was extremely biased towards the government, but I called that program almost every night to; attack the policies of the government, challenge his views, oppose the arbitrary detention of the opposition members without charge, call for their release, complain about food shortages etc.

I even organized a team of women to operate from the JLP headquarters, to saturate that program with our dissenting views!

It was only when I bumped into deputy JLP leader Pernell Charles some years later, that he told me how much that activity by us women had boosted the morale of the detainees. (Charles had been a very popular deputy leader of the JLP who was immediately detained the day the State of Emergency was declared. He was kept in solitary confinement for 11 months, only to be released without charge after the 1976 elections were held.)

When I first met him, I was warmed by his profuse praise for us women for having used the radio waves nightly, to shore up the spirits of the political detainees by, calling for their freedom and condemning the government for detaining them for political reasons only.

He said, after the first few weeks, just about everyone but us forgot about them while they were locked up in the nasty jails.

In addition, I set up a *paper organization* called "*Women Against Exploitation*" and fired off news releases on just about every issue, condemning the government on a regular basis for everything!

All this while also organizing my party branch at the grassroots level.

THE JANUARY 1979 GAS DEMONSTRATION

The straw that broke the proverbial camel's back and quickly mobilized the country in which people were tired of the hardships including; the violence, constantly escalating prices, frequent power cuts, the devaluation of our currency, and shortage of basic foods, was when the government announced that there would be further increase in the price of gas.

Increases on petroleum prices have always had an all-encompassing effect on everything, as transportation is a significant factor in all costs.

Already, we were having regular gas price increases, some caused by OPEC action but most, due to our dollar being constantly devalued because of the inefficiencies of the socialist system.

This latest escalation was due to the government increasing the *taxes* on the product, in a country that was already immensely over-taxed, with citizens getting very few benefits for the level of taxes being paid. (taxation without representation!)

When that latest increase was announced in mid-week, although we were few in numbers, we the youthful members of the NPM, decided that we had enough and were going to stage a demonstration the following Monday. We selected as our gathering spot; the Square now called *Mandela Park* in honor of the great Nelson Mandela himself.

This square is in the middle of Half Way Tree, which is basically mid-town Kingston and is an area through which most working people in the city must traverse.

A few days before the planned demonstration, we went to the JLP headquarters and told some senior party officials what we were planning, but were cold-shouldered.

However, we were later contacted by Douglas Vaz, a Member of Parliament in one of the more active constituencies. He told us he liked the idea and invited us to come to his party office on the Saturday, to update his constituents on our plans.

Enthusiastically we agreed and when we arrived at his office, there were around three hundred people there.

We explained to all present what we planned to do and most sincerely vowed to join us.

Convinced that we would have a great turnout, we then painted placards, on which we had numerous messages, *condemning the price increases, food shortages and other distressing economic practices* of the government. We then hid them in the Park close to where we planned to gather.

I then had two young children, Thor 8 and Michele 6, but I had a lady assisting me at home so I could be involved in political activity. We still lived in Spanish Town, St. Catherine, on the farm where we once cultivated rice.

At around 6 am the Monday morning, I jumped on my small 50 cc Suzuki motorcycle and rode to Kingston to join the others at the square.

Lo and behold however, when we were ready to start demonstrating at 7 am, there were only *ten other persons* there to march and parade with the numerous placards we had prepared.

Disappointed, we waited and waited for the masses to arrive, thinking it was only a matter of *Jamaica Time*. No one else turned up however.

About half an hour later, we were encouraged by one of the other members of our small group to grab the most relevant placards and start marching on the sidewalk.

Full of trepidation for we knew that protesters were often violently attacked by government agents, we hesitantly ventured out, everyone but me walking up and down on the sidewalk with placards while singing and chanting.

I couldn't leave my bike unprotected however, so started to push it up and down between the traffic, begging those motorists who would listen, to help me buy some gas, as the increased price threatened to put me on my feet permanently!

While most people nodded their support or honked their horns approvingly, they were just not prepared to park and join us in any protest. I now think we were not getting any support initially, because most people were genuinely nervous about their physical welfare.

Further, it was well known that persons could lose their jobs for any type of dissent. Even if persons worked in the shrinking private sector, they had to be careful what they did in public. For many owners insisted that their workers keep a low profile and stay out of politics as they were afraid they could lose access to foreign exchange to keep their struggling businesses afloat.

As the minutes passed by slowly and very few people joined our demonstration, it was extremely demoralizing, for we had been assured of such strong support the Saturday before.

After about an hour, we decided to pack it in, when suddenly we saw a bus full of passengers, barreling towards where we marched. As the huge bus could not maneuver easily through the slow traffic, caused by so many drivers slowing down to look at us demonstrators, it almost came to a full stop near us.

Although the bus stop was nowhere close, it was as if it slowing down to a crawl, was a signal for numerous passengers to exit. For the door suddenly flew open and people poured out. That was when a few young men ran over to where we were gathered and asked how they could get placards to march with us.

Suddenly, I saw a young man pull an ice pick from his pocket, plunge it into one of the bus's tires. He then walked slowly around the huge vehicle, repeating the same action until all the tires were damaged and it was totally immobilized!

Naturally, with the huge bus blocking that major corridor, all traffic coming down Hope Road, immediately came to a stop.

Since other motorists couldn't drive through, within minutes, people started to abandon their own vehicles, thus further disrupting the area.

Some came over to curse us demonstrators for disrupting their lives while others happily congratulated us for the initiative and joined in, leaving their cars parked right where they were. For now, they had no fear of losing a day's pay from their jobs, as they had a good excuse, *the blocked thoroughfare in Half Way Tree!*

This abandoning of vehicles and hordes of people gathering with us on the eastern side of the square, soon spread to the northern, western and southern sections, locking down the Half Way Tree corridor totally.

We were overwhelmed by the turn of events and by mid-morning, someone who was listening to radio, announced that the demonstrations and road blocks were reportedly spreading island-wide.

Soon, excited reporters were sending in stories from all over the country, about how people were using everything they could find; their bodies, huge boulders, trees, old cars, old appliances, anything, to block the roads in just about *every* major town in Jamaica.

Success more than we could ever have anticipated!

At around 11 am, I decided to travel back to Spanish Town to check on my young children who had been left at home with the helper, but even I, on my small bike, had to plead at two intersections, to be allowed through the road blocks on the thirteen mile journey home.

In fact, if I hadn't loudly declared that I was among the young people who started the protest in Half Way Tree, they would not have removed the boulders from a major intersection to let me through, without me first paying some money!

That lock down of Jamaica to protest the conditions in the country, became so successful that it lasted for *three days*. For by mid-day, the opposition saw the strategic importance of the mass protests, thus mobilized some of its activists to jump into action to help organize more road blocks or to ensure that those in place remained intact.

By the second day, most residents in the capital city, solved the problem of being unable to commute by simply staying home in silent protest while others went into the streets to ensure that the roads remained sealed.

Also, business operators and school administrators had appreciated the gravity of the situation on the first day combined with the determination on the faces of protestors, so they thought it wise to air announcements on radio informing all, that their establishments would be closed until further notice.

That helped the cause.

So, the road blocks continued island-wide throughout day two.

That was when I had a face-to-face confrontation with an actual ***USSR KGB agent***!

I, along with a couple friends, were manning the Constant Spring Road corridor which runs from a northerly direction through Half Way Tree Square to downtown Kingston.

We didn't have anything to do but entertain each other as both cars and people not involved in the demonstrations, were off the roads. For no one wanted to endure the hardships they had suffered the day before, trying to get home after abandoning their vehicles in many instances.

Suddenly we saw a lone car proceeding slowly down the road towards us, so immediately jumped into action to stop it. The vehicle was being driven by a white man, which caused us to instantly become even more alert, as we figured he might have been a Cuban.

As we approached the car, the driver held up *a single crutch* saying in halting English that it was an emergency, as he was on the way to the hospital.

Overcome by sympathy, we were just about to let him through when I noticed that the license disc pasted on the windshield had "*Embassy of the USSR*" written on it!

That was like waving a red flag in front of a bull, for the Russians and Cubans were the sworn enemies of us *freedom-loving* Jamaicans, as we considered them a direct threat to our lives and liberty.

Seeing a hostile agent in the flesh therefore was like getting a gift from God.

As if working on a cue, we all rushed to the driver's side determined to drag him out of his car and give him a thorough whipping. For clearly, this was a spy using the *crutch story* as a ruse to get through the road blocks to assess what was happening!

Our rapid change of mood and hostile lunge, made him aware immediately that we had seen through his subterfuge, so quickly, he slammed his car into reverse, floored the accelerator and sped off backwards up the road before we could even open his door!

By day three, the government had enough of us and sent in the army, their armed goons and their gestapo (police) to beat up people, teargas groups, break heads and dismantle road blocks wherever they were.

Even where they saw groups of people gathered, just watching the situation but not participating in road blocks or protests, they tear-gassed or used other means to chase them away.

Many of the terrorist squads were led by senior officials from the ruling party. Where the police were not directly involved in beating up and teargassing people, they looked on approvingly as the political thugs rained blows on us demonstrators.

The reports of brutal assaults on, and injury to demonstrators all over the island by the security forces and armed gangs affiliated to the ruling party, inspired many unbiased journalists to file and disseminate reports, not only locally but also with the international press and even Amnesty International.

Even many years later, occasionally I would run into quite a few people who still have visible scars of the beatings they received on that day.

Of course, there were some people who remained extremely upset at the inconvenience the three days of road blocks had caused them personally. Quite a few even told me how angry they were with *me* personally, for messing up their lives.

One of those persons was my own late mother, who all her life, had been an unwavering supporter of the government and the Manley family in particular!

She had driven to Kingston from St. Elizabeth (around 100 miles) to conduct business and had planned to return home the same day but because of the island-wide road blocks she couldn't.

She ended up having to stay in Kingston with my mother-in- law, who was her best friend.

So, I received a long lecture from her about the disruptive turn my life was taking and how inconsiderate I had been, not to have at least warned her of our plans to bring the country to a halt.

Poor me, for I had no such plans nor any idea that the simple demonstration we had schemed to mount by walking around with some placards, could have blossomed into such a monstrous event

But that is what happens when there is wide public discontent. For that demonstration caused by a small tax increase on gasoline was only the straw that broke the proverbial camel's back.

After the road blocks had been removed and most people terrified into seeking refuge in their homes, the prime minister went on radio and television to deliver a conciliatory speech, promising to roll back the taxes on petroleum.

But the anger in the country about everything including the presence of the Cubans and the shortage of basic goods was too much to bear, so attitudes changed and hostility towards the government soared radically for the rest of the year.

This caused even more regular unrests to break out in communities at the drop of a pin, making it impossible for the government to run the country effectively after that.

THE AFTERMATH

After the widespread manifestation of the unpopularity of his policies which the three-day demonstrations symbolized, Manley recognized that he had lost the authority to rule. So he announced that the general elections would be held on October 5th 1980, one year before it was constitutionally due.

That election which brought the socialist threat to an end, was the *bloodiest* election in the history of Jamaica.

Starting on Nomination Day in February through to Election Day, the guns never ceased barking one day or night, as the street violence which had been ever-present for around three years, increased everywhere in *ferocity and intensity.*

This not only caused more than 800 people to be killed in 1980, but also, thousands were injured. (As a matter of comparison, the death toll during the year leading up to the 1976 elections, was 162).

In addition, homes island-wide, belonging to supporters and activists of both parties, were burnt to the ground or severely damaged and even police stations fired on, while in the streets, JLP and PNP supporters not only shot at each other but anyone who they thought stood in their way.

Among some innocents who were caught in the crossfire, were 153 old ladies who resided at a home for the indigent called Eventide Home.

They were *burnt to death* when the home was deliberately set ablaze on May 21st that year.

To date there is no credible explanation about *who* did it or *why*. What is known is that the fire was set by men shooting wildly.

Another heart-wrenching murder was that of two, innocent young children in Top Hill, in St. Elizabeth. This occurred in October 1980, as Manley was touring the area with a group of his supporters.

According to the reports at the time, his devotees were heckled by supporters of the JLP candidate who was himself doing a walking tour of the same area.

The PNP group which was led by *the Prime Minister himself,* started to chase the detractors who sought refuge in a nearby home. The pursuing mob then charged the house and thinking their "enemies" were hiding under a bed in one of the rooms, fired shots wildly underneath.

When the smoke had cleared, it was discovered that it was the two young children who lived there who had been hiding under the bed and they had been shot and killed.

Tombs were subsequently erected prominently on the side of the main road near the spot where they were murdered, as a constant reminder of the day *when violence rocked that quiet, deep rural community.*

While the constant violence which was being perpetuated by the both sides continued, the shortage of basic foods, fueled so much discontent everywhere, that daily, a growing number of members of the public joined the frequent demonstrations against the government which became more paranoid as the days passed.

One knee jerk reaction to the constant discontent was their arrest of some members of a fledgling, insignificant party called the Jamaica United Front Party. Their leader and 27 members of the army, all of whom the government claimed were involved in a coup to overthrow them, were detained.

However, all were quickly freed as this had only been part of the continued effort by the government to keep the country on edge with their constant cry of *"destabilization."*

The murders, arson and other vicious acts of violence, forced all who could, to seek refuge overseas in droves, just to try and keep their families safe.

Although I did not live in the city which by then had become the prime killing field in the region, being a political activist and on the front-line so to speak, I started to feel my young children and I could be vulnerable.

However, I had only recently returned to live in Jamaica after three years in freezing Canada, so really did not feel I should leave my very beautiful island so a bunch of socialist thugs could enjoy it!

As the civil war progressed though, there were two murders, one extra chilling and one which struck home, which made me decide very quickly that the time had come for me to get my young children *out* of Spanish Town as it was too close to the violent capital city.

The first was a report about the spine-chilling murder of a young woman, who though some eight months pregnant, was still a political activist. Her body was found in a gully somewhere near Spanish Town Road and the baby had been cut from her stomach and thrown down beside her!

When I heard about it, I was sick to my stomach for days, as I just could not comprehend how, despite our political differences, we had developed such hatred and coldness towards each other that such a vicious act could have been perpetuated against a woman.

It made me even start to wonder if some politicians were giving their foot soldiers coke or some other mind-altering drug, to numb their senses, thus causing them to carry out such atrocities without compunction!

The other horrific incident was the murder of a couple I had just met at a party the Saturday night before.

The wife had been a long-serving PNP activist, who worked for years on the campaign of Manley's deputy prime minister.

Like so many people who hated the government's welcoming of hundreds of Cuban soldiers to our shores and the socialist system that was destroying our economy, she and her husband had switched allegiance and immediately started to work with the opposition JLP, in the same constituency.

When I was introduced to them at the party, we struck up an instant friendship as we had so many experiences in common to share, mainly about now we were treated by former friends and associates after having been an activist in one party and moving over to the other almost immediately.

I therefore could not believe my ears when I got a telephone call close to mid-day on the very next day, informing me how they had both been murdered in the wee hours of the morning, after returning from that party.

Although their house was fully grilled, it was reported that the assassins had spent quite a long time sawing off a section of the steel grills. Apparently on hearing them working on the outside, they sought refuge under their bed but that did not save them, as they were found there, dead and hugging each other tightly. Each had numerous wounds from high powered weapons all over their bodies.

That one really struck home and sent a streak of fear straight down my spine, as I had only been speaking to them a few hours earlier.

At that time, my mom still lived in the community where I was born, quiet, remote Malvern in the parish of St. Elizabeth, far away from Kingston.

However, Malvern was only about ten miles from Southfield where Manley and his goons had killed the two young children a few weeks before.

That was considered an aberration though, as the murder was committed by gunmen from Kingston, whom Manley had taken along on his trek into the country.

So, I still felt my children would be safer in faraway Malvern and insisted to my ex-husband that it would be the safest place for us to send them, until the war was over.

As there were only a few house telephones in remote Malvern, it was not too easy to get a message to her, so we took the hundred-mile journey home. When we explained our concerns, she was only too happy to have them living with her.

In fact, she said she had considered suggesting it to us, but hesitated as she was sure we would not want to be parted from them.

We then went to the nearby Munro Prep and had them registered to attend school there.

It literally broke my heart to have to return home without them, but what choice did I have?

It was the most painful and depressing decision I have ever had to make in my life.

While they loved visiting their grandma, when we told them we had to leave them there for a while,

hey cried hysterically but I could not comfort
them in any way, as I too cried uncontrollably.

We tried to visit often, but because of the gas
shortage at the time, sometimes it was weeks
before we could see them again.

Every visit ended with the same traumatic scenario
at the parting. For, it was as if a cold hand grabbed
my heart each time we had to drive away as we all
wept uncontrollably.

As difficult as this was however, we just had no
choice and as fate would have it, that immediately
turned out to be indeed a wise decision.

I was at that time, probably the heaviest sleeper in
the world, as, except when my young children's
cries of discomfort reached my ears, nothing else
could wake me up.

A few weeks after we took them to the country, I
was alone at home at the farm and even now, recall
the details vividly.

I had been listening to a radio call-in program and
remember hearing the *10 pm* time signal so must
have fallen asleep soon after.

My ex-husband who was a night owl, had not yet
returned home from Kingston but although the
house was isolated and I was alone, I never really

felt afraid. So usually, by the time he got home, I was in dreamland.

When I was rudely wakened that night, I thought I was having a nightmare in slow motion and real color, for there was a man in a mask *on top of my ex-husband*, right there beside me in my own bed!

I remember dazedly asking what was happening for I guess I still thought I was dreaming. It must have been the tone of my ex-husband's voice that brought me to reality for he shouted, "Don't you see a man on top of me?"

Immediately I became conscious enough to realize that indeed it was not a dream for there was blood all over the bed.

The entire bedroom was in total confusion because while I slept, the two men had been wrestling for control of the gun, right there on the bed beside me, while bullets were being expelled wildly. Even the radio, which had been on a bedside table when I was listening to it, was entangled with other stuff on the bed beside me.

During the fierce struggle, my ex-husband had been chopped and shot once.

Thankfully though, while he and the man struggled for control of the gun, two bullets had found their mark in the chest and stomach of the intruder, so by the time I got awake he was barely alive.

In all, five shots had already been fired right in the bed beside me and the gun was empty by the time I jumped into action and succeeded in pulling the barely-struggling man off my ex.

When he fell on the floor, my ex jumped up and grabbed the gun from the bed as it had slipped from his hand during the struggle. It was only when he pointed it at the man on the ground and pulled the trigger, that he realized that all shots in the barrel had already been fired.

Even then, I still had not woken fully from my trance, then I saw all the blood over my partner and realized that he too had been shot.

Thinking he might bleed to death, I don't even remember if I changed my clothes but grabbed him and shouted that we must get to the hospital.

That is when a pall of fear swept over me, for it occurred to me that we would be attacked and killed when we exited the house, as quite likely, the intruder had an accomplice outside.

It was pitch black, as my ex had turned off the exterior light when he came home and there were no street lights in that deep rural community.

Further, our closest neighbor was probably half a mile away so in the best of times we never saw any lights from their home.

Fortunately for us, there was no accomplice lurking outside, so somehow, I got my wounded ex into the car and, although I don't recall anything else, I clearly managed to drive the more than four-mile journey to the hospital.

All I know is that later in the morning, I was told that I had arrived at the emergency room screaming and covered in blood.

Amazingly too, I seemed to have driven all the way to the hospital, clutching the gun in one hand and a machete in the other!

I assume officials at the hospital must have summoned the police as the next thing I remember is that I was surrounded by quite a few of them and questions were being fired at me from all sides.

My ex was not badly hurt as it turned out that the chop on his foot was not very deep and the bullet had gone straight through the palm of his hand without damaging any bones, so he could be treated and sent home.

The police accompanied us back to the farm and by the time we arrived, the sun had begun to rise and it was quiet and peaceful outside.

I reluctantly entered the house but flatly refused to go into my bedroom, remembering immediately the scene we had left inside. As I sat alone in the living room, a policeman came out and told me that they found a dead man in a mask, on the ground beside our bed.

It was only after intensive inspection of the crime scene, that the police assisted by my ex-husband, were able to piece together, a picture of what had occurred in the dead of night, for remember I had been totally out of it.

Firstly, our assumption that the man had on mask because he either worked for us or was known to us, was incorrect as my ex could not remember ever having ever seen him before and from the description I got, I did not know him either.

Then it was revealed, that the machete that was used to attack my ex as he lay in the bed, belonged to us!

Years ago, when we were touring Mexico after leaving Toronto, we had purchased a shiny machete in a beautifully designed leather case with Mexico inscribed on it. We had brought it home, never sharpened it but had instead hung it on the wall of our living room, as a souvenir.

It was the man's possession of *our machete* and a knife found wrapped in newspaper on his dead body, that made us realize that he had entered the house and had most likely been hiding inside for some time, before my ex returned home.

The police therefore concluded that when he broke into our home, he had only a knife as a weapon. On seeing the shiny machete, he must have figured it would be a more lethal weapon, so wrapped up his knife in newspaper and secured it in the waist of his pants.

Thank heavens that machete had never been sharpened!

When the criminal heard my husband arrive, he waited hidden for a while, giving him what he figured was enough time to fall asleep, before invading our room wielding the machete.

It was during the police's inspection of the crime scene that it suddenly hit me how insightful the decision to send our children away, had been.

For it is through *their* room that the intruder had entered, after removing a window pane.

That information made me shudder at the thought of what he could have done to them when he found them alone, unprotected, sleeping peacefully in their beds, if they had not been sent away.

The police further surmised that the reason he remained hidden waiting for my ex to fall asleep was because it was really the gun he had come to steal, for it was well known in the area that my ex owned one.

Luckily, he had not yet fallen asleep or maybe had been awoken by some sound, he couldn't remember.

He however always slept with his gun under his pillow and on glimpsing the shadow lunging on to the bed, quickly pulled the weapon and fired.

Fortunately, the dull machete missed its main target but connected with his foot. His first bullet however hit the assailant squarely in his chest. So, he fell on top of my ex, and the other four bullets were expelled as they both fought for the possession of the gun. During that melee, two more hit the intruder and one caught my ex-husband in his hand.

As they had wrestled intensely beside me though, with the shots being fired wildly, I slept peacefully. My partner only realized the gun was empty, after the man fell on the ground and he was able to retrieve it from the bed where it had fallen during the struggle.!

Don't ask me either, how I drove with a weapon in each hand, for clearly, I had operated on *automatic pilot* all the way!

Only god knows how I got through that night but I did and lived to tell the tale.

There was an interesting development which surfaced the next day, which I now find hilarious, though at the time I was in no mood for humor.

For in no time a story spread far and wide, that I *the sleeper,* was a heroine.

This happened as the tale about me arriving at the hospital carrying a gun in one hand and a machete in the others while escorting my injured husband to get medical treatment, spread far and wide and became the main topic of discussion for days.

That narrative, immediately created the impression that I had killed the man.

No matter how I denied it to those who approached me congratulating me for having overcome and killing the intruder, they wouldn't believe it! Some even insisted that they had got the details from the police, so it was true that I shot the man!

Nothing could be further from the truth.

A mystery that the police helped us clear up, was why the intruder thought we might recognize him, thus his wearing a mask.

It turned out that he had worked at the gas station in the town that was owned by a friend of ours and that is where we did our business.

The owner told us that he had been fired many months ago, when he was arrested by the police on a gun charge. A few days before he broke into our home, he had been released on bail.

He added that since it was well known that my ex had a gun as he was always doing target practice on the farm, he concluded that the man had broken into our home to steal the weapon. For he later heard from a good source that after he was released, he had declared that he wanted a gun to kill the policeman who had arrested him and seized his weapon.

After that night, we went to stay with relatives in Kingston and I swore that I would never return to live in that house in Spanish Town, but after about a month away, decided to give it a try. For the entire night though, I could not sleep, as every time I closed my eyes, I saw a man in front of me in a mask.

We therefore returned to live in Kingston, this time taking up temporary residence with my mother-in-law, until we could sort out our lives.

CONCLUSION

On Election Day 1980, despite the constant violence; unnecessary tear gassing, the shooting up of communities and polling stations, it did *not* prevent approximately *87%* of the electorate from turning out. For the vast majority of Jamaicans were determined to get rid of Manley, to *remove forever,* the socialist threat and the possible domination of our island home by Cubans and the USSR.

There were however reports of massive corruption and voter fraud being carried out by activists from both parties in many constituencies. There was ballot stuffing, stealing of votes and voter intimidation at the polling stations, but it was also clear that the results reflected *the will* of the majority, as they coincided with the regular polls which were done leading up to the elections. Those polls had been conducted by the most credible pollster in the Caribbean, Professor. Carl Stone, and published in the Gleaner newspaper.

As much as I had come to dislike the turn Michael Manley made in the 70's and his determination to *sell out* the interest of Jamaicans to the Cubans, I say without apology that he was the most charismatic, effective political leader and motivator we have ever had.

Problem was, he sought to lead the country in the wrong direction!

Had Manley, with his great charm and ability to convince people to do just about anything, retained the *liberal capitalist economic policies* that we were accustomed to and put the interest of Jamaica *first,* like the late *Lee Kuan Yew* did in Singapore, our little country could have become the richest, most dynamic and progressive island in the Western Hemisphere. For during the early 70's, Lee Kuan Yew had visited Jamaica and marveled at the beauty of the country and our abundance of natural resources.

Singapore has a slightly larger population than Jamaica and they live on 277.65 square miles of land space whereas Jamaica's land mass is 4243 square miles. We also have far more valuable raw materials, than Singapore does too. In 1972, *Singapore* had a GDP of US $2.72 billion which by 1980, had grown to $11.98 billion. By comparison, during the socialist experiment in *Jamaica,* our GDP only rose from $1.8 billion in 1972 to $2.68 billion in 1980!

Of note too, is the fact that when Jamaica got independence in *1962,* its GDP was $777.71

million, so in the first ten years after independence when the country had sensible liberal capitalist economic policies, GDP growth increased by almost **250%** despite our main non-agricultural industries being in their infancy. After the backwards socialist economic policies were implemented, our growth barely crawled at less than 100% over the next 10-year period!

Also, due to Manley's corrupt socialist policies, the poor became much poorer, for as in Venezuela today, *high inflation, poor health care, frequent power cuts, factory closures, basic food shortages* and *a massive brain drain,* became the order of the day.

In the meantime, the political rulers lived in splendor as they lauded their vulgar material wealth and status over us. For while we could hardly get the basics to send our children to school, stories about the luxuries that the children of politicians openly displayed, were widespread as were the stories of the fabulous parties hosted by their parents.

A never-ending legacy of that period too, is the continued violence that has become so entrenched in the society, that today, my country is frequently listed among the five most murderous countries in the world, on a per-capita basis.

While we were able to ward off the threat of Cuban/USSR domination via the ballot box in Jamaica, in the tiny eastern Caribbean island of Grenada, in 1983, it took a rescue mission by US troops, assisted by soldiers from the *English Speaking Caribbean islands*, to save that small island from the from socialist threat, which is a fate worse than death!

Incidentally, several Jamaican far left activists, had been involved with the *treasonous politicians* in Grenada, who murdered their elected Prime Minister, Maurice Bishop and accommodated the Cuban/USSR imperialists.

While I specifically have no evidence, stories abounded that the JLP got assistance in terms of weapons and strategic advice and even money, from the American CIA.

In light of the fact that those who tried to sell out our country to the eastern bloc, were armed and financed by the USSR's KGB and the Cuban *DGI,* I reiterate even now, that had the CIA or any other US agency not assisted the JLP in that undeclared civil war that raged between 1977 and 1980, the freedoms we accept as normal today, would not have been preserved.

I therefore thank President Jimmy Carter for assisting us to retain our freedoms.

For I have visited Cuba four times, the last time being in 2014. On that occasion, it was to meet my cousins who I had only recently discovered were born there and all still lived in Holguin province.

Although the natural beauty of that country which I observed from my first visit and which was what always spurred me to return, cannot be destroyed, *socialism* has made life there intolerable for the people.

For today, *poverty is pervasive, corruption and prostitution are rampant* as people turn to any means necessary to survive.

No wonder, for decades; thousands of people have risked their lives in rickety boats to escape from that island.

In short, the socialist system is designed to condemn everyone *but the leaders*, to a life of poverty and deprivation.

For under that heavy-handed government-controlled system, it is a small band of politicians and bureaucrats who decide *who gets what when and where.*

Freedom of choice no longer exists, so that it why socialism can only survive under a dictatorship.

In a free market, people determine where they want to spend their money, based on the best deals that competition presents, so individuals are much better off and happier.

And I say this without fear of contradiction, for I visited *East Germany* twice before the Berlin Wall was torn down. I can't help but recall how going from one country to the other, was like going from the light into darkness as one traveled from West to East.

And remember, the US had no sanctions against East Germany for that is often the excuse given by *socialist apologists* for the disastrous conditions in Cuba.

I notice too, that this same refrain is being used by some, to explain the *catastrophic* economic conditions in once wealthy Venezuela, which have been brought about by socialist policies.

According to the United Nations, this situation has caused some *four million people* to have fled the Madura regime so far, seeking refuge abroad!

By outlining in detail the trauma we endured because of our socialist experiment, I am explaining to readers why I *personally* find that philosophy so *unpalatable*.

However, I am not so presumptuous as to assume that other persons in larger, more developed countries would go through the same suffering we did, although I cannot but often equate my own experiences to what I see thirty million Venezuelans now enduring.

Remember too, **Venezuela,** which has *the largest known oil reserves in the world,* was probably the most liberal and prosperous country in South America until it adopted socialism in **1998**.

I cannot imagine that a large, diversified, developed, capitalist economy like America's, could ever be transformed into a socialist one though, even with the best efforts of backward thinkers like *millionaire Bernie Sanders* and his surrogate *Alexandria Ocasio-Cortez,* who in March 2019, described *capitalism* as *irredeemable.*

A Gallup poll in May 2019, found that four in ten Americans support *some form of* socialism but I *doubt* that these respondents were looking at socialism in its *pure form.* I suspect that most are confusing normal *social policies* as exist in the Scandinavian countries, other parts of Europe and in Canada, with socialism which has *a definitive economic policy.* For I hear this confusion being expressed a lot, not only in personal conversations, but also in public debates and coming from political platforms.

That is why the last chapter of this book is dedicated to outlining some of the *normal* social programs that that are taken for granted, in the top ten capitalist countries where people say, they are the happiest.

What is important to remember though, is that *socialists have no monopoly on dictatorship*, for even when politicians are democratically elected, they can take a country in a direction that the voters never intended.

The great philosopher **Plato**, considered by many as the founder of western political thought, warned in **The Republic** written 380 BC, *that democracies eventually degenerate into tyrannies.*

This is not necessarily true but we must never forget that *Hitler was democratically elected.*

In Europe, at this time, we also see the dangerous *autocratic trends* in both *Hungary* and *Turkey* where their leaders, Orban and Erdogen, were also democratically elected.

It is my impression, too, that if the Democrats did not become the majority party in Congress in 2018, the dictatorially-inclined Donald Trump, would have been able to manipulate both the senate and congress to enact *legislation to stifle the free press,* which he and his supporters constantly deem to be "enemies of the people."

Who knows too, he could probably even have bullied the weak-kneed Republican legislature into amending the constitution to allow him to remain as *president for life!*

For Trump has shown every inclination that he would like to go in that direction.

Plato also observed that the most important qualities in a *statesman are* **truthfulness** and **expertise,** but both these qualities are absent in the leadership of the USA today.

The great philosopher was also on target when he warned that demagogues get their start by taking *over a particularly obedient mob.*

That is exactly what Trump has done with the base of the Republican party.

No wonder so many people, even high-profile ones in that party, like *Anthony Scaramouche,* Trump's former press secretary and *Joe Walsh,* are beginning to see the light and the eminent danger of having a man who is clearly racist and unstable, not only in the White House but also with nuclear weapons at his disposal.

Walsh, a former Representative from Illinois who now admits that he helped create the *monster*, describes his former hero as; *nuts, erratic, cruel, bigoted*.

We must therefore never cease to remember that only vigilance by the citizens can effectively protect a country from socialism and other forms of repression.

PART 11
RACISM

TRUMP IS A RACIST

Every time I see one of the frequent debates on American television about whether Trump is a racist or not, I remember the wise words by **Maya Angelou;** "*When people show you who they are, believe them*!"

For hasn't Trump demonstrated throughout his adult life that he is an unapologetic racist?

I need not go back too far into his actions as a private citizen, to draw that conclusion!

I am from the Caribbean so have never experienced American-style racism. I have always heard about the atrocities though and seen some blood curdling documentaries on television.

However, over time I had assumed that with the Civil Rights successes of the 1960's and 1970's, Americans had virtually thrown off the shackles of racism.

That myth was shattered when Trumpism became a reality.

Now, the USA is once again, *openly* extremely dangerous and challenging for non-whites.

For the powerful US president has given leadership and legitimacy to undying racists, most of whom had previously tried to disguise their toxic philosophy.

This reality did not only shock me, but apparently many persons throughout the world.

No wonder in February 2017, John Bercow, the powerful speaker of the house of parliament in Britain, America's closest ally, declared that he would oppose Trump addressing parliament during a state visit to England, because of his country's opposition "to racism and to sexism and support for equality before the law."

One reason why so many of us were caught off guard was because we naively thought that when the great USA elected its first African American president, **Barak Obama**, in 2008, it meant that they had finally decided to bury that terrible legacy forever.

Obviously, the very opposite was true. So, Trump's election has now empowered the millions of closet racists who became incensed that the progressive majority had elected a black man to run the country stolen from the Native Americans.

It was clearly not an aberration therefore, when powerful Republicans like Mitch McConnell were openly declaring that they would do everything to ensure that Obama failed as president.

In her autobiography entitled, **"Becoming"** Michelle Obama wrote "Weeks before the inauguration, the conservative Radio host Rush Limbaugh boldly announced, 'I hope Obama fails.' I'd watched with dismay as Republicans in Congress, followed suit, fighting every effort to stanch the economic crisis, refusing to support measures that would cut taxes and save or create jobs."

And lest you forget, when Obama became president, the US economy was collapsing faster than it had during the onset of the Great Depression.

According to the US Labor Department, the job loss in December 2008, a month before he was inaugurated, was a whopping 524,000!

When Trump promised during the campaign to reverse just about every policy the Obama presidency had instituted, even the poorest of the poor, who, thanks to Obama, were getting decent health care for the first time in their lives, cheered.

So, swaddled by racism were these fanatics, that they even embraced that promise to their own detriment and that of their children.

Those *Trumpists* were prepared to have the entire America, including themselves, suffer for electing a black man.

Clearly in their sick minds, whatever it took to erase all evidence of the country ever having a president of color, had to be done!

So no, Trump is not responsible for the fact that maybe up to sixty-three million adults in the USA are closet or openly white supremacists.

As someone who has never been coy about spewing his racism from the rooftops, he simply became *their legally elected leader and messiah.*

It was not surprising therefore to see that of the 11 confederate states, he won 10: *Alabama, Arkansas, Florida, Georgia, Louisiana, Mississippi, North Carolina, South Carolina, Texas, West Virginia.*

And as if on cue, in November 2016, a black church in Mississippi was burnt to the ground and 'Vote Trump" spray painted on one of its walls.

Naturally, David Duke fully endorsed the new leader.

David Duke is a former leader and still an extremely influential spokesman for the despicable, bloodstained Ku Klux Klan.

That well-supported, white supremist organization, is best known for bombing black churches and killing children.

After Trump's inauguration, Duke declared; "We are determined to take our country back. We are going to fulfill the promises of Donald Trump. That's what we believed in, that's why we voted for Donald Trump. Because he said he's going to take our country back. That's what we gotta do."

Trump earned his spurs as a racist leader, long before he even showed an interest in running for office.

He secured it when he wholeheartedly adopted and expanded on the sinister "birther" campaign against Barak Obama in 2011.

In that campaign, it was claimed that Obama was not an American but indeed born in Africa.

When documents were provided proving the birther conspiracy was a lie, the racists upped the campaign with other versions alleging that; Obama's published birth certificate was a forgery, that his actual birthplace was not Hawaii but Kenya, even claiming that that he became a citizen of Indonesia in childhood, thereby losing his US citizenship.

This entire campaign was a hateful and vitriolic reaction by white supremacists to Obama's status as the *first African-American president of the United States*.

Trump in 2016, claimed he no longer believed the birther conspiracy, but by then the damage had been done and he had achieved his goal.

If there was still any doubt about the president being totally racist, that was erased when on July 14th 2019, he tweeted with reference to four female democratically-elected congressional women of color who had been critical of him; "So interesting to see 'Progressive' Democrat Congresswomen, who originally came from countries whose governments are a complete and total catastrophe, the worst, most corrupt and inept anywhere in the world (if they even have a functioning government at all), now loudly and viciously telling the people of the United States, the greatest and most powerful Nation on earth, how our government is to be run. Why don't they go back and help fix the totally broken and crime infested places from which they came. Then come back and show us how it is done. These places need your help badly, you can't leave fast enough."

Of the four women that this racist tweet was directed at, three were actually born in the USA and one had lived in the country and been an American citizen longer than Trump's wife, Melania!

In *the book of Trump* and his racist followers though, no non-white person can *ever* be an American!

According to the president himself, his ratings among Republicans voters increased by 5%, after his tweet telling the four congressional representatives of color to go home!

All doubt has now been removed too, that the party he leads is just a pathetic racist reflection of their leader.

So, today, in 2019, almost the entire Republican Senate is white, with only one *ineffective* junior senator of color there and in Congress the scenario is the same.

The Trump regime has confirmed 150 judges at the time of writing and no doubt they are overwhelmingly *white*. For when the first 87 were confirmed, an investigation was done, and of that number, there was only one African-American and one Hispanic, no doubt to give them a racial alibi!

For no politician in this era, no matter how stupid and despicable, wants to be without that precious *racial alibi.*

See how quickly Rep. Mark Meadows of North Carolina was able to draw on one!

In March 2019, in a sick move to try and defend the president against the charge levelled by Michael Cohen, that Trump, his former friend and client was a racist, Rep. Mark Meadows quickly found a *rare* black person who worked with the Trump organization, to put on display.

Thankfully, not too many people of color are still prepared to continue being held up as the Republican's *Uncle Tom* however. Recently, a former high profile one jumped ship.

That was, Gregory Cheadle, the man Trump referred to at a rally as '*My African-American.*

He seems to have finally recovered enough self-respect to leave the GOP, telling PBS in September 2019, that he has become fed up with the party as they treat black people as a "political pawn" while running a "white agenda."

Well, as they say, *its better late than never* and who knows, maybe one day, all people of color who now support the GOP, will regain their self-respect and refuse to be continually used as *racial alibis*.

Living outside the USA, I personally only started to become aware of how much the Trump campaign had begun to change the racial atmosphere in the USA, by empowering closet white nationalists, when in 2015, my grandson who attended college near Tampa, Florida, called to say he wanted to leave that university as he no longer felt safe there.

This was not only because numerous confederate flags had started to appear in dorm windows all over his campus but worse, one night returning from the nearby university town, he and his friends saw a group of between four and five men lurking around on the roadside near the campus, dressed in Ku Klux Klan garb.

He lost an entire semester because he had to leave that part of the state for his safety, to relocate to another university in Miami.

My daughter too saw the immediate effect of Trump's campaign at the school she taught in a suburb of Denver, Colorado when huge crosses were erected on the front lawn of her elementary institution, after a black principal was hired.

The principal who had been born, educated and worked all her life in the state, told me some months later, that she had never experienced anything like that before in Colorado, which made her feel so unsafe in her own backyard, for the first time in her long life.

Trump's empowerment of white supremacist became even more dangerous immediately as he was elected president, starting at an event branded as the Charlottesville *rally,* by some in the media.

However, that gathering in Charlottesville, Virginia, in August 2017, was in no way as innocuous as a rally, for it was planned to intimidate, murder or otherwise harm non-racists and it certainly did.

This event was spawned from the white supremacist cult called, *Unite the Right,* which decided to protest the removal of a statue of Confederate General Robert E. Lee.

For because he was nothing but a traitor and undeserving of a statue in the public square, the city council of Charlottesville had earlier in the year, voted to have it removed and placed in a museum.

This is a section of a report of those events as carried in the Washington Post August 13, 2017. "Chaos and violence turned to tragedy Saturday as hundreds of white nationalists, neo-Nazis and Ku Klux Klan members — planning to stage what they described as their largest rally in decades to "take America back" — clashed with counter protesters in the streets and a car plowed into crowds, leaving one person dead and 19 others injured.

Hours later, two state police officers died when their helicopter crashed at the outskirts of the town. Officials identified them as Berke M.M. Bates of Quinton, Va., who was the pilot, and H. Jay Cullen of Midlothian, Va., who was a passenger. State police said their Bell 407 helicopter was assisting with the unrest in Charlottesville. Bates died one day before his 41st birthday; Cullen was 48."

After that brutal event, President Trump who has never been able to bring himself to condemn white terrorism, described the perpetrators of those killings, including Nazis and KKK members, as "very fine people."

This endorsement of racist groups by the powerful republican leader, has been music to the ears of his faithful followers.

More joy has also come to them via Trump's hateful verbal assault against immigrants of color, some of whom are even seeking asylum.

He describes all non-white would-be immigrants as; "invaders who are infested with diseases."

The verbal campaign against immigrants of color, has stirred up such hatred against people who don't look like the president and his racists followers, that individual white terrorists, have taken it as license to murder innocent human beings.

So, in October 2018, when a white extremist shot up a Jewish synagogue in Pittsburg, Pennsylvania, killing eleven worshippers and injuring dozens of others, he gave as his reason for the vicious attack, his belief that Jews were assisting *"invaders"* to come to the USA.

Even in distant New Zealand, his hateful rhetoric resonated, for in his manifesto, the Australian white supremist who shot up two mosques in February 2019, killing fifty worshippers and injuring another twenty, ranted against immigrant "invaders."

His most hateful language against immigrants from the day he came down the escalator, has been against *Mexicans* who he has termed *rapists* and *very bad people*, time and time again.

Is it any wonder therefore that this reprehensible rhetoric empowered a white supremacist to drive more than six hundred miles *to hunt down* Mexicans who he realized shopped at a Walmart in El Paso, Texas?

There, he slaughtered 22 on the spot, while injuring another 24.

His vitriol and poisonous salvos against immigrants of color has continued unabated to the point where it even emboldened his surrogates to cruelly *tear away babies* from their mother's breasts, even where these brown people, in keeping with the terms of International Law, were seeking *refugee status* in the USA.

The brutality of this anti-white immigrant campaign has shocked the entire civilized world for there is no doubt that it is based solely on plain outright racism.

For while disparaging immigrants of color, the president was simultaneously ruing the fact that more Norwegians are not trying to migrate to the USA.

Clearly Trump does not know that Norway is consistently rated among the top **five** happiest countries in the world while America barely makes t in the top 20. So why would any resident of Norway be rushing to migrate to the USA!

As if this flagrant campaign against people of color trying to the get to the USA was not harsh enough, Trump even added insult to injury by referring to entire countries including Haiti and some in Africa, *as shithole counties*.

Whereas this new low was surprising to some, apparently it was quite a habit of his, as his long-time personal lawyer and former friend Michael Cohen, testified at a public hearing in Congress, that in an effort to "put down" Obama's presidency, Trump once asked him (Cohen) if he had ever seen a country that was run by blacks that was not a shithole country!

The over 3.5 million Puerto Ricans, though being American citizens, have also been treated like *shithole people* by the Trump administration. For after the island was devastated by Hurricane Maria in September 2017, which caused some 4,000 people to lose their lives and left the entire island in despair, his response was totally disrespectful and callous.

In an article published in Newsweek in October 2017, under the headline "Trump Treating Us Like Dogs,' Say Puerto Ricans" one complainant was quoted as saying "The president's behavior led some Puerto Ricans to say he was treating them like second class citizens."

According to a report in The Toronto Star, Joel Isaac, a Puerto Rican who moved to New York three years ago, but who has most of his family still living on the island, was quoted as saying; "He arrives with a smile on his face, makes fun of the situation, shows no empathy, lies and lies on camera as he does 24-7. And then throws paper towel rolls to people in need, as if he was playing 'Go Fetch with dogs."

Frances Alvarado, a Puerto Rican living in N. Carolina, was cited thus; "Does he think this is a show? A game? The first reaction that I had: why is he throwing things to Puerto Ricans like we're animals?"

The article further stated;

"Trump has been criticized for his administration's reaction time to deliver relief efforts on the island and for taking two weeks to visit the disaster zone where 3.5 million American citizens live. The president visited Texas and Florida within days after they were respectively hit by Hurricanes Harvey and Irma in August and September."

In a warning to those who try to excuse Trump's blatant racism and ignore white supremacy, in

August 2019, President George W. Bush's chief speechwriter and syndicated columnist wrote this heart-wrenching column;

'I had fully intended to ignore President Trump's latest round of racially charged taunts against an African American elected official, and an African American activist, and an African American journalist and a whole city with a lot of African Americans in it. I had every intention of walking past Trump's latest outrages and writing about the self-destructive squabbling of the Democratic presidential field, which has chosen to shame former vice president Joe Biden for the sin of being an electable, moderate liberal. But I made the mistake of pulling James Cone's 'The Cross and the Lynching Tree' off my shelf — a book designed to shatter convenient complacency. Cone recounts the case of a white mob in Valdosta, Ga., in 1918 that lynched an innocent man named Haynes Turner. Turner's enraged wife, Mary, promised justice for the killers. The sheriff responded by arresting her and then turning her over to the mob, which included women and children. According to one source, Mary was stripped, hung upside down by the ankles, soaked with gasoline, and roasted to death. In the midst of this torment, a white man opened her swollen belly with a hunting knife and her infant fell to the ground and was stomped to death.'

God help us. It is hard to write the words. This evil — the evil of white supremacy, resulting in dehumanization, inhumanity and murder — is the worst stain, the greatest crime, of U.S. history. It is the thing that nearly broke the nation. It is the thing that proved generations of Christians to be vicious hypocrites. It is the thing that turned normal people into moral monsters, capable of burning a grieving widow to death and killing her child.

When the president of the United States plays with that fire or takes that beast out for a walk, it is not just another political event, not just a normal day in campaign 2020. It is a cause for shame. It is the violation of martyrs' graves. It is obscene graffiti on the Lincoln Memorial. It is, in the eyes of history, the betrayal — the re-betrayal — of Haynes and Mary Turner and their child. And all of this is being done by an ignorant and arrogant narcissist reviving racist tropes for political gain, indifferent to the wreckage he is leaving, or the wounds he is ripping open.

Like, I suspect, many others, I am finding it hard to look at resurgent racism as just one in a series of presidential offenses or another in a series of

Republican errors. Racism is not just another wrong. The Antietam battlefield is not just another plot of ground. The Edmund Pettus Bridge is not just another bridge. The balcony outside Room 306 at the Lorraine Motel is not just another balcony. As U.S. history hallows some causes, it magnifies some crimes.

What does all this mean politically? It means that Trump's divisiveness is getting worse, not better. He makes racist comments, appeals to racist sentiments and inflames racist passions. The rationalization that he is not, deep down in his heart, really a racist is meaningless. Trump's continued offenses mean that a large portion of his political base is energized by racist tropes and the language of white grievance. And it means — whatever their intent — that those who play down, or excuse, or try to walk past these offenses are enablers.

Some political choices are not just stupid or crude. They represent the return of our country's cruelest, most dangerous passion. Such racism indicts Trump. Treating racism as a typical or minor matter indicts us."

Trump's bigoted rhetoric and slander is not only bringing comfort to racists in the USA, for on August 23, 2018 he even retweeted a false claim by a South African rightwing racist group that there were "Widespread Attacks on White Farmers in South Africa."

This false claim was naturally hailed on the same day by the *League of the South*, described by Wikipedia thus; The League of the South (LS) is a white nationalist, Neo-Confederate, white supremacist organization, headquartered in Killen, Alabama, which states that its ultimate goal is "a free and independent Southern republic."

While many GOP leaders have confided to a few people in the press that they abhor Trump's rhetoric, the fact that the GOP leadership has been openly condoning or endorsing it with their silence, has indicted the entire Republican party.

THE REPUBLICAN PARTY IS NOW FULLY RACIST

So, not only is the leader of the powerful USA is an outright and unapologetic racist, but he even boasts that his real ideology is *nationalism*.

Readers will of course recall that the most notorious nationalist in history of the world, was none other than Adolph Hitler, the man who many white supremacists and neo-Nazis in the USA, still publicly declare is their hero!

It should horrify everyone therefore, that not only is the president of the most powerful country in the world, the enabler of dangerous white supremacist and a nationalist, but also that the party he leads, has by silent consent, shown that *they have embraced fully, his sick ideologies.*

I say the world should be horrified, because whereas Trump can be removed in a few years, the well-established and once respectable Republican party, will probably be around for many more centuries thus influencing millions of Americans in the future*!*

Since Trump became president, the chilling indications of where the country is heading, is all too clear.

According to the *Southern Poverty Law Centre*, "The number of hate crimes in the United States in 2017 topped a previous high, with law enforcement reporting 7,175 incidents — an uptick of *17 percent* over the five-year high reached in 2016."

But the intentions of the Trump administration are to encourage instead of stamp out white supremacist's actions. This has been made clear from day one, as outlined in an article in the on-line news feed *Latest.com* dated May 27, 2017 entitled "*White House Budget Slashes Funding to Fight Domestic Terrorism.*

It stated in part; "The White House budget proposal features cuts to almost everything but defense spending, in light of the conflict against terrorism. However, the budget also cuts a program aimed *at reducing domestic extremism, most of which is white nationalist related.*

The program, known as 'Countering Violent Extremism' is aimed at challenging the ideas of extremists and preventing radicalization."

Naturally white supremacists have been emboldened, and worse, none no more so than those who have been hiding in plain sight in police forces throughout the USA leading to the murder of unarmed black people by the police reaching alarming proportions!

It is as if hardly a week passes since Trump was elected, without some white police killing an unarmed black person with impunity and worse, often getting away with it.

No place seems safe for black men these days, not even the home of one's close family. For in Sacramento, Stephon Clark who was *unarmed*, was shot 20 times by the police and killed while in his own grandmother's backyard!

In an article entitled, "There are huge racial disparities in how US police use force" written by German Lopez and published in *Vox* on Nov 14, 2018, the author cited statistics from the Guardian, stating in part;

'Racial minorities made up about 37.4 percent of the general population in the US and 46.6 percent of armed and unarmed victims, but they made up 52.7 percent of unarmed people killed by police."

Deadly bias by the American police is also attracting much comment overseas, as exemplified in the *BBC's* question, "Why do US police keep killing unarmed black men?"

In the report, Sam Sinyangwe, a researcher and activist who started the Mapping Police Violence project, stated in part;

"I'm 24 years old. I'm a black man. It's incredibly depressing to see people just like me who have been killed.

I started the project to provide answers in the wake of the shooting of Mike Brown. It's very heavy to read these stories, and yet it feels like the right work to do. It's important.

There are statistics on all kinds of violent crimes. And yet, when it comes to people being killed by police officers, there's no data on that. So, a light bulb went off in my head. I looked at two crowd-sourcing databases which collected all the names. I then went through the media reports listing each of those people who were killed."

It continued; "In the aftermath of Ferguson (when the unarmed teenager Michael Brown was killed), there was this big question 'Is this a pattern, is this an isolated incident?' What [my data] shows is that Ferguson is everywhere. All over the country you're seeing black people being killed by police." The youngest recorded was 12, the oldest 65. More than 100 were unarmed. Black people are three times more likely to be killed by police in the United States than white people. More unarmed black people were killed by police than unarmed white people last year. And that's because black people are only 14% of the population here."

When you compare how keen the white police are to gun down unarmed black men in comparison to their actions towards white mass murderers, white supremacist terror groups and even a white cannibal, there can be no question about the overall unfair and prejudiced treatment *based solely on race*, being meted out by many hiding in the police force in the USA. These extreme examples should suffice:

On 21 June 2015, the web site *The Source* raised eyebrows by publishing an article headlined "Police Chief Says Dylann Roof Was Taken to Burger King Shortly After Arrest."

Roof, a white supremacist was taken into custody alive and well and treated to burgers after he carried out a terrorist attack, murdering *nine black churchgoers* during a prayer service, at the historically significant Emanuel African Methodist Episcopal Church in downtown Charleston, South Carolina, in what was clearly a hate crime.

Can you in your wildest dreams, imagine an armed black man who went into a church, and murdered white people at prayer being taken alive, much less being treated to hamburgers by the police afterwards?

Even a white cannibal in Florida was treated with respect and taken safely into custody, a far cry from how innocent black men are often handled by the police.

In that case which occurred on August 16, 2016, according to *UPI;*

"A college student was arrested Monday for the alleged brutal killing of a couple after police found him eating the face of one of his victims.

Police said Austin Harrouff, 19, a student at Florida State University, randomly killed 59-year-old John Joseph Stevens III and 53-year-old Michelle Karen Mishcon -- daughter of former North Miami Beach mayor Jeffrey Mischon -- in their garage and driveway, and also stabbed a neighbor who tried to stop the attack."

It's not only in policing where this type outright racial bias exists but also in the justice system, for according to the *Anti-Defamation League*, white supremacists commit most of the extremist's killings. However, they only make up only 30% of the prison population which is swollen with black men who have done nothing more than have some marijuana in their possession.

Further, The United States Sentencing Commission reported in November 2017, that black male offenders received sentences on average *19.1 percent longer* than similarly situated white male offenders.

Don't expect that this injustice can be eliminated soon either, in fact I expect it to worsen exponentially with the rapid nomination of judges by the Trump regime and the eager confirmation by the all-white senate.

How many of these newly nominated judges endorsed by Trump and his all white senate are of the same ilk as judge Mark Hulsey in Florida? He was forced to resign in 2017, when he faced impeachment.

According to the *Washington Post*, on accessing court documents, they verified that Hulsey made comments about African Americans, such as, "They could go get back on a ship and go back to Africa."

Citizens have also to be vigilant as to whether the Trump judicial nominees will try to reverse long standing legislating outlawing segregation in schools, for if the article in *Slate Magazine* is correct, there are indications that they may be heading in that direction.

In that feature published in April 2019 entitled; *Trump's Nominees Won't Say if Brown v. Board of Education Was Decided Correctly*. I quote the relevant section; "One year ago to the day, one of Donald Trump's nominees to a seat on the Eastern District of Louisiana, Wendy Vitter, sat before the Senate Judiciary Committee and declined to say whether Brown v. Board of Education—the 1954 ruling that struck down the "separate but equal" doctrine in public education—was correctly decided. In response to a question from Sen. Richard Blumenthal on the topic of Brown, Vitter replied, "I don't mean to be coy, but I think I can get into a difficult, difficult area when I start commenting on Supreme Court decisions—which are correctly decided and which I may disagree with. Again, my personal, political, or religious views I would set aside—that is Supreme Court precedent. It is binding. If I were honored to be confirmed, I would be bound by it, and of course, I would uphold it."

At the time, it seemed that Vitter and other nominees were willing to go further than we had ever believed possible to make the claim that Brown was indeed precedent while avoiding saying that they agreed with one of the most widely accepted Supreme Court decisions of all time. Ten years ago, such a maneuver would have been unthinkable. As Perry Grossman and I noted last year, "At his Supreme Court confirmation hearing in 2006, Samuel Alito called [Brown] 'one of the greatest, if not the single greatest thing that the Supreme Court of the United States has ever done.' Only a year ago, Neil Gorsuch said at his confirmation hearing that Brown was a 'seminal decision that got the original understanding of the 14th Amendment right.' What changed in the time between Gorsuch and Vitter has nothing to do with whether Brown is still good precedent. What changed is that judicial nominees are carving a path toward saying that they needn't be bound by any precedent, and also that every precedent is now on the table. When judicial nominees say, as they now regularly do, that Brown is a precedent of the court, what they are really saying is that a case that was decided and that it's the law until it's reversed. That is a truism—it is a description of what is. It is also a departure from a standard that existed until quite recently."

And as I write, there is a strange development in a case involving a white supremacist who worked with the coast guard. He was found with a huge arsenal of arms and ammunition, *a hit list* and reems of ramblings containing racial slurs.

In the report of his arrest in February 21 2019, KLAS 5 tv reported these disturbing facts;

A Coast Guard officer suspected of drawing up a hit list of top Democrats and network TV journalists spent hours on his work computer researching the words and deeds of infamous bombers and mass shooters while also stockpiling weapons, federal prosecutors said Thursday.

Lt. Christopher Paul Hasson, 49, was ordered held without bail on drug and gun charges while prosecutors gather evidence to support more serious charges involving what they portrayed as a domestic terror plot by a man who espoused white-supremacist views.

Hasson, a former Marine who worked at Coast Guard headquarters in Washington on a program to acquire advanced new cutters for the agency, was arrested last week. Investigators gave no immediate details on how or when he came to their attention.

Federal agents found 15 guns, including several rifles, and over 1,000 rounds of ammunition inside his basement apartment in Silver Spring, Maryland. In court papers this week, federal prosecutors said he compiled what appeared to be a computer-spreadsheet hit list that included House Speaker Nancy Pelosi, Senate Democratic Leader Chuck Schumer and presidential hopefuls Sens. Kirsten Gillibrand, Elizabeth Warren, Cory Booker and Kamala Harris. Also mentioned were such figures as MSNBC's Chris Hayes and Joe Scarborough and CNN's Chris Cuomo and Van Jones.

In arguing against bail Thursday, federal prosecutor Jennifer Sykes said Hasson would log onto his government computer during work and spend hours searching for information on such people as the Unabomber, the Virginia Tech gunman and anti-abortion bomber Eric Rudolph.

Sykes said the charges so far are just the "tip of the iceberg" and called Hasson a "domestic terrorist" who appeared to be planning attacks inspired by the manifesto of Anders Behring Breivik, the Norwegian right-wing extremist who killed 77 people in a 2011 bomb-and-shooting rampage."

A judge however has decided to grant bail!

In an astounding story on Friday 26th April 2019, it was reported by CNN that the judge now rules that he would be granted bail as he had not committed a crime.

Interestingly, his defense attorney contended that the language full of hate and racial slurs found in his notes were no worse than President Trump's so it was not criminal!

Could this defense by the lawyer have found favor with the judge, had this terrorist not been a white racist? Can you imagine what would be the fate of a Muslim found with such dangerous weapons and a narrative outlining plans to assassinate people?

THE RACISTS ARE EVERYWHERE

If you think this rabid racism is now only pervasive in the white house, the senate, the judiciary and police force, think again.

It has always been on the fringes and under cover, but since Trump once again gave it legitimacy, it is being openly displayed all over, at every level of the society, to the point where sometimes it is it is even downright laughable.

Like in the case of the pathetic republican mayoral candidate Kimberly Barnette who in May 2017 in Charlotte N. Carolina, urged people to vote for her as she is "Republican, and smart, white and traditional, according to an article in the Huffington Post!

She clearly knows exactly Republican voters want to hear.

Not all lower level republican politicians make such trite racists comments as they seek to woo the base though, for some others are downright *brutal, disrespectful* and even *cold-blooded.*

The entire campaign about making *America great again caters* directly to those hankering after the glorious past when whites lolled around, living off the fat of the land while black slaves were used to cater to their every need, at the pain of death!

I consider the United Health Care ad on tv, as a subtle reminder of those "great day." For in the ad we see the happy, carefree, white lady 'busily' walking the dog, going to the gym and enjoying life while the harried black worker strives to help her find a convenient time in her busy schedule, to do her own health check-up!

How symbolic of white privilege, for as Kate Smith sang decades ago, *that's why darkies were born.*

Yup. The message is, since America was great in the days when black people did the back breaking work while white people lolled around, when Trump takes the country back to those days, *America will be great again.*

Clearly Shane Bouchard, the Republican mayor of the second largest city in Maine remembers those days with great glee, that's why he could joke in March 2019, that "elderly black people were antique farm equipment," as reported in *The Sun Journal.* For in the good old days when America was great, it was black people who were doing the backbreaking field work that mechanical farm equipment does today. So, to him and the millions of others of his ilk, a black person is nothing but an antique farm equipment.

This innate racial attitude is so sickening that if one had read about it in a fictional work, one would wonder how someone could be so cruel as to even think of human beings in that manner.

But these sentiments and the degrading ones his president often uses, are neither fictional nor fake news.

Not all the sickening memories that leading Republicans have been publicly expressing are as harmless though, for how can we ignore Republican Sen. Cindy Hyde-Smith of Mississippi, hankering for the days when lynching of black people was part of the entertainment enjoyed by many whites in her state.

In 2018 during the elections, she proclaimed with reference to one of her staunch supporters; "If he invited me to a public hanging, I'd be on the front row," according to the Washington Post report on November 2018.

According to the NAACP, Mississippi alone accounted for *an eight of the lynching committed between 1882-1968.*

This love of lynching is clearly not only a historical fact but clearly still a fond memory by many in the south.

Look at this story out of the Alabama, as reported by the *Montgomery Advertiser* on February 24th, 2019 entitled 'Alabama newspaper editor calls for Klan return to 'clean out D.C.'

"The editor of a small-town Alabama newspaper published an editorial calling for "the Ku Klux Klan to night ride again" against "Democrats in the Republican Party (sic) and Democrats (who) are plotting to raise taxes in Alabama.

Goodloe Sutton, who is the publisher of the Democrat-Reporter newspaper in Linden, confirmed to the Montgomery Advertiser on Monday that he authored the Feb. 14 editorial calling for the return of a white supremacist hate group. Asked to elaborate what he meant by "cleaning up D.C, Sutton suggested lynching.

"We'll get the hemp ropes out, loop them over a tall limb and hang all of them," Sutton said.

When asked if he felt it was appropriate for the publisher of a newspaper to call for the lynching of Americans, Sutton doubled down on his position."

The everyday attacks on people of color for absolutely no reason except racial bias, continues unabated. Even black motorists on the roads are singled out, something that caught the attention of the *Daily Mail* in the United Kingdom which in April 2019 in an article entitled "Black motorists are 20% more likely to get pulled over than white drivers, a new Stanford University study finds." It expanded;

•	Stanford University analyzed 93 million traffic stops between 2001 and 2017

•	Analyzing data from 21 patrol agencies and 29 different police departments, authors of the study say there is evidence of 'widespread racial discrimination'

•	Black drivers were also found to be searched nearly twice as often as whites, despite the discovery of drugs or guns being more common on a white motorist

•	Revealing a quite significant racial bias, the study echoed a sentiment that African-Americans and other people of ethnicity have long shared

•	Authors of the study suggest the damning results may help to contextualize the violence behind high profile police stories, such as Walter Scott's shooting"

In the workplace too, dangerous biases are now being openly displayed, including a number of incidents where nooses are being placed in areas where blacks are working.

Less lethal but just as discriminatory, is the increase in the number of employers telling black people how they can wear their hair while no such restrictions are placed on white workers.

The increase in complaints about this has forced the New York City Commission on Human Rights to denounce the policy in February 2019 and published guidance to fight race-based hairstyle discrimination under the local New York City Human Rights Law.

Even, the burning of black churches has once again surfaced as a favorite sport among white supremacists. Far more lethal though, are the incidences of race-based acts of domestic terrorism and mass murders which almost weekly shock the nation. It is very significant though, that in the midst of these increases, the republican administration seems determined to *encourage* these acts. For why else would they cut the budget to fight this scourge?

On August 19, 2019 the *Fiscal Times* carried this piece.

"The Los Angeles Times reports that, despite evidence of a rise in domestic terrorism incidents involving white supremacists, "the Department of Homeland Security, which is charged with identifying threats and preventing domestic terrorism, has sought to redirect resources away from countering anti-government, far-right and white supremacist groups."

The Times and NBC News report that a former DHS official testified before Congress in June 2019 that the department had made significant cuts since 2017 to the office handling domestic terrorism, reducing a staff of 16 full-time employees and 25 contractors with a total budget of about $21 million to fewer than 10 full-time employees and an operating budget of $2.6 million, is extremely troubling and clearly demonstrates the fact that the Republican government is determined to fuel an increase white supremacist action.

ECONOMIC APARTHEID

Racism has not only been physically and psychologically devastating to people of color, but also, anyone who doubts that America is wealthy because of decades of practicing racism and genocide, needs to watch the You Tube documentary *"America's Big white Secret."*

Revealing too, is the article published in Forbes magazine on September 1st, 2019, entitled; *"America's First Bond Market Was Backed By Enslaved Human Beings."* by Pedro Nicolaci da Costa.

Today, there are many white people in the United States, who though not considering themselves racists, silently criticize black people for lagging economically, even suggesting it is because they have failed to take advantage of the opportunities available to people residing in the "land of the free".

However how many have stopped to understand how much *they* have benefitted economically only because of their *color of their skin?*

Conversely, how much do they know about how blacks have continually *suffered economically* because of the color of *their skin*?

It is easy to be cavalier when one does not
understand how decades of *economic apartheid*
has affected the entire black race over the years,
putting whites at a natural and unfair advantage.

I won't even bother to go into too much detail
from as far back as the days of slavery to remind
those readers that during slavery, their white
ancestors all benefitted *directly or indirectly* from
the labor of the slaves.

Economic apartheid continued to flourish
unchanged when slavery was abolished, for
emancipation left most blacks *homeless, cashless
and uneducated.*

Worse records show that even after the Civil War,
black individuals who had a little land, wealth or
other property, were often stripped of these *by
white, heavily-armed exploiters* who in many
instances, were *protected by the white
establishment.*

During World War 1, blacks were promised that if
they *put their lives on the line* and went to war,
they would be compensated. *They were not* but
white veterans were. Even most of those injured in
that war, were deprived of disability pay while
their white counterparts weren't.

In 1944, the GI Bill was enacted to guarantee benefits to veterans of World War 11. However, In the piece entitled "**African Americans and the GI Bill**" in *Wikipedia*, it states in part;

"The G.I. Bill aimed to help American World War II veterans adjust to civilian life by providing them with benefits including low-cost mortgages, low-interest loans and financial support. African Americans did not benefit nearly as much as White Americans. Historian Ira Katznelson argues that "the law was deliberately designed to accommodate Jim Crow".[1] In the New York and northern New Jersey suburbs 67,000 mortgages were insured by the G.I. Bill, but fewer than 100 were taken out by non-whites.[2][3]

Additionally, banks and mortgage agencies refused loans to blacks, making the G.I. Bill even less effective for blacks.[4] Once they returned from the war, blacks faced discrimination and poverty, which represented a barrier to harnessing the benefits of the G.I. Bill, because labor and income were immediately needed at home.

Most southern university principals refused to admit blacks until the Civil Rights revolution. Segregation was legally mandated in that region. Colleges accepting blacks in the South initially numbered 100. Those institutions were of *lower* quality, with 28 of them classified as sub-standard. Only seven states offered postbaccalaureate training, while no accredited engineering or doctoral programs were available for blacks. These institutions were all smaller than white or non-segregated universities, often facing a lack of resources."

Now if those who put their lives on the line for the United State of America, could be treated so unfairly, can you imagine how the federal government and financial institutions treated *black non-combatants*?

The huge black population you see swelling the ghettos of the big industrial cities in the United States, are a direct result of the financial apartheid that blacks were subjected to after world war two.

For whereas white veterans and those working in factories during the boom years, could get mortgages to enable them to move out into the suburbs, blacks were deprived of loans, strictly on the color of their skin.

To add insult to injury, the few who managed to get a loan, were not allowed to live in white suburbs so they ended up in the overcrowded under-resourced ghettoes in the large cities that you see today.

It was from situations such as this that many wealthy ghetto landlords were created and enriched. Some who are influential people in the government today, got their start as real estate entrepreneurs who took advantage of blacks who could get no-where outside of the *overcrowded inner cities* to live.

It is also telling that in 2017, Pew research found that 84% of black people still felt they were treated differently from whites when applying for mortgages!

The separation between where blacks and whites generally live as a result of economic apartheid, naturally affects their children and the level of education they receive.

In January 2018, City Lab exposed that; "In many U.S. cities, enrollment in urban public schools is dominated by kids from lower-income households, often black and Latino. More affluent white urbanites who've moved to gentrifying city neighborhoods often send their children to private or charter schools, because of fears about underperforming local public schools."

That's right, local public schools that most children of color in major cities attend, *are underperforming,* because they are under resourced by the government!

The main reason why these schools are under-resourced, is because funding is based on property taxes. Property taxes in the suburbs are naturally far higher than those in the urban centers, so how can people ever escape from poverty when the inequalities in economic opportunities, housing and education continually keep them down?

What is happening to black pregnant women too, is designed to make the progress of the race even more difficult, for in September 2019, an article written by *Amy Roeder* in Harvard Public Health, exposed in great detail, the shocking difference in treatment of black and white women, which has resulted in a situation where ; "African American women *are three to four times more likely to die during or after delivery than are white women.* According to the World Health Organization, their odds of surviving childbirth are comparable to those of women in countries such as Mexico and Uzbekistan, where significant proportions of the population live in poverty."

There is still no fairness in the area of employment either for a new Demos/NAACP report, found that retail employers pay Black and Latino full-time workers *just 75 percent* of the wages of their white peers!

An article in *Glamour,* written by Meena Harris and published on August 22, 2019, also states in part; "For women overall, it takes about 16 months to make what a white man makes in 12. But for black women, that number is higher. It takes 20 months to even out!"

Kamelia Harris painted an even more depressing picture in a recent debate when she revealed that today, black women generally earn only about 60% of what white men are paid to do the same job."

What was most shocking however, was the revelation made in the article in *Rolling Out* by Terry Shropshire, entitled "Average White high school dropout earns more than college grads of color" in which it was disclosed that; "For Black families and other families of color, studying and working hard is not associated with the same levels of wealth amassed among whites. Black families whose heads graduated from college have about 33 percent less wealth than white families whose heads dropped out of high school. The poorest white families—those in the bottom quintile of the income distribution— have slightly more wealth than black families in the middle quintiles of the income distribution. The average black household would have to save 100 percent of their income for three consecutive years to overcome the obstacles o wealth parity by dint of their own savings activity." This information was garnered from research done by the Pew Research Centre.

So, discrimination designed to keep non-whites from ever catching up, continues everywhere unabated and it explains how continued *racial apartheid* in America, is responsible for the many violent, overcrowded inner cities that are home to millions of people of color, making the poverty cycle almost impossible to break.

The now *fully racist Republicans* will therefore probably do everything to ensure that things get worse, never better, for it is not their belief that blacks, *from whose blood and sweat a wealthy America* was built, should ever be given *any* rewards.

FREE AND FAIR ELECTIONS NEEDED

Racism is just too destructive, *physically, psychologically* and *economically,* for even a wisp of this *debilitating* philosophy to be still tolerated now much less in the future.

It is therefore incumbent on upholders of human rights and justice to reject *via the ballot* in 2020, the very possibility of it continuing.

The Republican leaders, have recognized that outside of their racist base, their evil policies are being resisted.

So, in the elections in 2018, when they saw the real possibility of their party being wiped out at the polls, instead of doing the practical and human thing, ie. tackle racism and adopt civilized policies, including the maintenance of health care for millions which Obama fought for, they instead adopted a program of *fraud and voter suppression* to try to hold on to power in Congress.

The most blatant examples of *extreme political mal-practices* during those mid-term elections, were found in *Georgia, Michigan, North Dakota and North Carolina.*

A few excerpts from the reports from independent media houses are quoted below;

<u>Georgia</u>

An article appeared in the October 2018 in *Salon* under the headline "Analysis: Brian Kemp has purged over 300,000 voters from Georgia rolls."

This article, exposed Republican Georgia Secretary of State Brian Kemp, for seeking to suppress the black vote ahead of the election, in which *he* was also a candidate.

In short, Kemp was not only running for the position of governor, but also, he was in total control of the election machinery for the state!

<u>Michigan</u>

According to a report in the *Detroit News* of Thursday April 25th 2019, in an article entitled; "Federal court: Michigan political maps illegally rigged to 'historical proportions," it stated— "Michigan must redraw legislative and congressional districts for the 2020 election because current maps drawn by Republicans represent a political gerrymander 'of historical proportions,' a three-judge federal panel ruled Thursday"

<u>North Dakota</u>

The *Bismarck Tribute* reported in its article entitled; "North Dakota tribal leaders highlight 'unfair' voter ID law in congressional hearing".

This article is written by Amy Dalrymple and published on April 16, 2019 states in part;

"North Dakota tribal leaders urged members of Congress Tuesday to protect Native American voting rights, highlighting a state voter identification law they said creates unequal access to the ballot box.

Representatives from four of North Dakota's tribal nations raised concerns to a U.S. House subcommittee about the state's law requiring voters to present an identification with a street address.

Many addresses on rural reservations are post office boxes and street addresses aren't assigned, tribal leaders said during a field hearing of the Committee on House Administration Elections Subcommittee. Simply put, it is a massive hurdle for many on Standing Rock reservation to figure out their actual residential address," said Charles Walker, judicial committee chairman for the Standing Rock Sioux Tribe."

The hearing held at Standing Rock, was one of several around the country the subcommittee is holding to gather evidence and testimony of *voter suppression* that will be used to inform future legislation.

<u>North Carolina</u>

The worst case of election fraud in the 2018 mid-term elections, was in North Carolina though. The excerpt below was taken from a New York Times story of the February 21st, 2019.

'North Carolina officials on Thursday ordered a new contest in the Ninth Congressional District after the Republican candidate, confronted by evidence that his campaign had financed an illegal voter-turnout effort, called for a new election. The unanimous ruling by the five-member Board of Elections was a startling — and, for Republicans, embarrassing — conclusion to a case that has convulsed North Carolina since November.

And it followed testimony that outlined how a political operative had orchestrated an absentee ballot scheme to try to sway the race in favor of Mark Harris, the Republican candidate. It is now the single undecided House contest in last year's midterms. Robert Cordle, the state board's chairman, cited "the corruption, the absolute mess with the absentee ballots" when he called for a new election.

All this came after months of inquiry into the conduct of a criminal who was employed by the Republicans to collect absentee ballots and evidence emerged that he and some of his cohorts tampered and changed some ballots!

And can you believe, in light of all this voter fraud outlined above not one person has been jailed?

However, in March 2018, *National Public Radio (NPR)* reported; "Texas Woman Sentenced *To 5 Years for Illegal Voting.*"

Naturally, that poor woman was black.

That very troubling report only demonstrated once again how black people are victimized by the justice system in the USA.

The person involved, a Ms. Mason, had been on a supervised release after spending three years in prison. For a time, she was even working for the state of Texas, St. John says. She was sentenced to five years for voting illegally although she contended that she was never informed of the state's voting restrictions on felons.

Isn't this also just typical of how the justice system works when racists hold the reins of power too, for in all the cases above, it was demonstrated how thousands and possibly millions were prevented from voting or fraud committed, yet not one of hose who perpetuated those crimes was even prosecuted much less jailed, while one poor little black woman who voted illegally, was sentenced to 5 years!

If people really want change to a democratic process and the rule of law, far more than the 57.9% of registered electors who bothered to go out to do their constitutional duty in 2016, must to do so in 2020. In addition, Americans owe it to *themselves, their children* and the rest of the world, to be vigilant, as what they do affects everyone on the entire planet!

So, voters must be careful that;

a) Racists, with the assistance of powerful hostile states like *Russia*, do not once again get away with imposing *their choice* for president on the country. For the Muller *report does confirm* that the lily-white Russians *did* in fact intervene in the democratic process to elect Trump as president of the powerful US.

And remember, this interreference by *that hostile power,* was welcomed by the Republicans, as apparently will be, any that they can extort out of the poor Ukrainians!

Now that the precedent has been set, I wonder what will the Republican's response, if sometime in the future, *a hostile non-white nation like China or Iran*, puts its spy agency at the disposal of a nominee from the Democratic or an independent party to help elect the president of the USA?

b) Citizens must become extremely vigilant to prevent criminal acts of voter suppression and voter fraud everywhere as took place in four states in which the Republicans 'won' overwhelmingly in 2016.

VIOLENCE IS A REAL POSSIBILITY

As terrible as the cases of voter suppression, fraud and external assistance by a hostile foreign state have been, what is really worrying is the *possibility that in the* upcoming 2020 presidential elections there will be election violence.

For there are indications that the Trump team realizes that if he is defeated, he faces the real possibility of being *prosecuted and imprisoned for criminal activities with which he cannot be charged, while being president.*

The likelihood of violence was first raised by none other than Trump's *longtime attorney and confidant*, Michael Cohen who testified at a public hearing in front of Congress in February 2019.

It was there the man who had once said he would take a bullet for Donald Trump, raised the specter of political chaos and even violence if the man he once served, failed to win re-election in 2020. For he told Congress that he feared there would *never* be a "peaceful transition of power."

More troubling, Trump *himself* added fuel to that possibility, in the eerie communication below, as interpreted by *Jack Holmes* in *Esquire* on March 14th 2019.

"This has been a banner week for democratic backsliding. On Wednesday, Donald Trump, American president, gave an interview to Breitbart the once-prominent right-wing content machine that was caught laundering white-nationalist propaganda into the mainstream. In the interview, he hits a familiar refrain—but ratchets things up a notch.

'You know, the left plays a tougher game, it's very funny. I actually think that the people on the right are tougher, but they don't play it tougher. OK? I can tell you I have the support of the police, the support of the military, the support of the Bikers for Trump—I have the tough people, but they don't play it tough—until they go to a certain point, and then it would be very bad, very bad. But the left plays it cuter and tougher. Like with all the nonsense that they do in Congress … with all this invest that's all they want to do is —you know, they do things that are nasty. Republicans never played this.'

Leave aside, for a moment, the scattergun syntax and the deeply preposterous idea the Republican Benghazi Party doesn't like itself a congressional investigation. This is the real deal: Here is the president hinting his political opposition could be met with force if 'they go to a certain point' certain point'? Impeachment? Defeating him in the 2020 presidential election?"

The threat of violence *must be taken very seriously*, for even if we disregard the above rhetoric, the reality is that several times during the 2016 elections, Trump did indeed encourage his followers to use violence!

Much more ominous, is the fact that since his ascendancy to the leadership of the Republican party, there has been a massive increase in white nationalist's terror groups and hate crimes, not only against African Americans, but also against Jews, Latinos, Moslems, Hindus and Sikhs.

Then there are the *kill lists* found in the possession of terrorist or at their abodes, containing the names of journalists, and politicians from the democratic party which often read like statements coming out of a Trump rally.

Of note too, is that despite this lethal trend, the republican government refuses to investigate and neutralize *white domestic terrorists*, in the same manner that they went after members of the equally dangerous terrorist overseas groups. This despite the fact that foreign inspired terrorism has been reduced radically, while domestic terrorism, inspired by white nationalism has increased dangerously.

From 2017, Tom Porter asked the question in an article in *Newsweek* entitled "White Terrorism' and Donald Trump: Why Has the President Slashed the Grant for Group Combating KKK?"

Also, writing for the *Fiscal Times* on the 16th August 2019, Yuval Rosenberg stated in part;

"The mass shootings in El Paso and Dayton that left at least 31 dead have raised questions among lawmakers and former officials about the Trump administration's efforts to thwart domestic terrorism, and the resources the Departments of Justice and Homeland Security are allocating toward that mission.

"We need to invest more — no question," Acting Homeland Security Secretary Kevin McAleenan said Tuesday on "CBS This Morning."

The *Los Angeles Times* also reported that, despite evidence of a rise in domestic terrorism incidents involving white supremacists, "the Department of Homeland Security, which is charged with identifying threats and preventing domestic terrorism, has sought to redirect resources away from countering anti-government, far-right and white supremacist groups."

The Times and NBC News report that a former DHS official testified before Congress in June that the department had made significant cuts since 2017 to the office handling domestic terrorism, reducing a staff of 16 full-time employees and 25 contractors with a total budget of about $21 million to fewer than 10 full-time employees and an operating budget of $2.6 million."

Does this sound like the actions of a government interested *in cutting or fostering domestic terrorism,* which today is almost entirely linked to the white supremacist ideology?

Additionally, there are some 300 million guns in the USA, the vast number of which seem to be owned by those committed to making America white again.

The writing is on the wall and those who prefer to ignore these dangerous signals, will most likely soon face a rude awakening.

PART 111

HAPPINESS

THE WORLD HAPPINESS REPORT

In the Declaration of Independence, Americans are told about having the right to life, liberty and *pursuit of happiness.* While I will not debate the first two, we need to look at how the USA is doing in the area of happiness.

The only system I know of that sets out to measure how happy people really are, is in the work done to compile an annual **World Happiness Report.**

This project came out of a resolution adopted in July 2011, at the UN General Assembly.

As a result, there is now a global survey ranking *156 countries* by how happy *their citizens perceive themselves* to be. It is published annually by the United Nations Sustainable Development Solutions Network.

The areas polled, using data from Gallop World Poll surveys are; *income, freedom, trust, healthy life expectancy, social support and generosity.*

The first results were published in April 2012.

At that time the USA was rated number *13* but since then, it has *fallen* to number 19.

Clearly the country is failing terribly in facilitating its citizens in their quest for *happiness*.

On the other hand, a little country like Denmark, has certainly found the formula, as when its citizens do not say they are living in the happiest country in the world, they are rated number 2.

That country has a very high tax rate but citizens are extremely happy with the social services offered, best being the high quality of health care and education.

What is amusing is the fact that if certain narrow-minded or ignorant Americans looked at the social services that Danish citizens take for granted, they would shout *socialism* from the rooftops.

Hopefully the prime minister of that country can help them to understand the realities of life.

I quote Lars Løkke Rasmussen, Prime Minster of Denmark;

"I know that some people in the US associate the Nordic model with some sort of socialism. Therefore, I would like to make one thing clear. Denmark is far from a socialist planned economy. Denmark is a market economy."

For further clarification, let me state that *a market economy is a capitalist economy.*

According to **AOC**, capitalism is irredeemable, but *that is an absolutely false statement.*

Whereas proper regulations can make capitalism work in the interest of all the people, *socialism can never do that*. For once politicians get their grubby hands on the *economic controls,* that is the end of private initiative and competition.

History is full of examples of countries where socialism was tried, but could only be enforced under dictatorships, as citizens are just not prepared to voluntarily tolerate the hardships caused by heavy-handed government control.

I therefore suspect that when Gallup found in June 2019 that *four in ten* Americans are looking favorably at socialism, they were being confused by the propaganda being spewed by the AOC's and Bernie's of the world.

Hopefully the prime of Denmark has helped them remove the scales from their eyes.

But one does not have to go as far as northern Europe to observe the distinctions, for the Canadians next door, who the records show have a much lower *per capita income* than their neighbors in the USA, consistently indicate via the same polls that they are more than *twice* as happy as Americans.

It is my opinion that the two most compelling reasons why Canadians say they are far happier than Americans are; *a)* because the government to the north, is far *more humane,* so they have extremely helpful social programs and *b)* to prevent the exploitation of the poor by the rich, their economy is far more regulated. So, among other things, *income inequality* in Canada is much lower than it is in the USA, as the *Gini* index indicates.

Take the main cause of private bankruptcies in the USA, they are chiefly due to medical expenses.

This was recognized by **President Obama** who quickly set out to deal with this horrific situation.

He introduced the *Affordable Health Care* act, to ensure that *all* Americans who need it, could have their health care covered by either *private* companies or a *government run program.*

However, since the Trump regime took power, they have tried several times to take away health benefits from sick people. When they failed through the courts, they used every means possible to *destabilize* that program.

It is not only the medical care that causes a heavy strain on American families, but also the ridiculously high cost of prescription drugs.

Interestingly, each year, hundreds of thousands of Americans cross the border to go to Canada to fill their life saving prescriptions, for a fraction of the cost at home. Why?

This is because successive *capitalist* Canadian governments, like many progressive governments around the world, *control the price that drugs* are sold and distributed for in their territories.

This is something Senator Amy Klobouchar, who is seeking the Democratic nomination, said she would do if elected president of the USA.

Even if she doesn't succeed in her quest, it is a wise, humane policy for the rich USA to adopt, to help alleviate the financial difficulties of its citizens, caused by health issues.

That is obviously also a positive step in assisting a vast segment of the American public in their 'pursuit of happiness.' And there is nothing socialist about facilitating affordable health care for one's citizens!

As if it weren't bad enough that the Trump administration is trying its best to destroy Obama's Affordable Health Care plan, they are even adding insult to injury by *removing* numerous regulations overseen by the Environment Protection Agency (EPA).

This they are doing to facilitate large, wealthy corporations so they can maximize their profits *at the expense of ordinary citizens.*

Not even water and food are exempt from this callous attempt by the Republicans to destroy people's health.

For now, *clean water regulations* introduced to ensure that corporations are not allowed to contaminate underwater sources, are being lifted.

Where food is concerned, in a report in *The Hill* in September 2019, it was revealed that the USDA (Department of Agriculture) has slashed the number of inspectors required at pork factories and according to *Human Rights Watch.*

Not only are consumers now at greater risk of consuming contaminated food, but also the *workers* at meat packing plants are being put at risk because, "The Trump administration is weakening oversight of chicken, hog, and cattle producers, and lifting limits on production speeds."

These attempts to neutralize necessary regulations, are designed to re-introduce *unbridled capitalism.*

This is unacceptable in the modern era, for these rules were designed to keep the population *healthy*.

While some propagandists will insist that regulations impede production in market economies, nothing could be further from the truth, for all sensible American administrations, have always implemented or enforced regulations to some degree, to protect consumers and prevent unnecessary pain.

In fact, it was the lack of proper regulations in the financial markets which led to the *collapse* of the economy under George Bush.

That disaster was only corrected after Obama put sensible economic policies in place.

Even *Warren Buffet*, one of the richest men in the world who describes himself as a "card carrying capitalist," is on record in a CNBC discussion in May 2019, as calling for *capitalism to be regulated*.

It is this recognition that regulations make the market economy run better and protect the weak from the powerful, why bodies such as the FCC, FDA, SEC. FDIC etc. were set up.

Had the regulations provided under the SEC not been enforced to break up the giant telecommunications company, *ATT* in the 1990's, the communication revolution which is benefitting millions of consumers, would not be a reality today.

Had the SEC not successfully brought a case against the *dominant* Microsoft in the 1990's too, the world would not be gaining from the services offered by companies such as Google and Yahoo today.

So those calling for dominant companies like Amazon and Facebook to be regulated and even broken up, are not *anti-capitalist* or *leftist* fanatics, but in fact people interested in fair competition and equity.

As businesspeople rarely ever put citizens' welfare first, government agencies must at times take companies to court, to curb their greed and protect the public.

Note the opioid crisis today and how rapacious pharmaceutical firms are being forced to pay for having destroyed hundreds of thousands of lives.

Action in the USA, against cigarette manufacturing companies that in the past, put profits above people's health, set the precedent for much of what you see being decided in the courts against some pharmaceutical companies today.

So, you see, market economies can be regulated to act responsibly and provide equity.

However, the government must have the will to do so.

Unfortunately for Americans, the Republican party is one that *caters to the greedy* and they consistently do everything to deregulate the economy at the expense of the majority.

No wonder Americans have become unhappier under the Trump administration.

Another reason why deregulation, detrimental *to the welfare* of the majority is so often implemented, is because of the *money-power* of lobbyists.

For under the USA's system, corporations with deep pockets can *bribe* politicians to do anything, even where it is totally harmful to the majority.

This is legal because the system of lobbying is flawed.

Look at the issue of gun ownership, something which has brought so much sorrow to millions of people as not even children in kindergarten are immune from being massacred by armed terrorists with high powered weapons of war.

For years, thousands have been calling for sensible legislation to thoroughly vet those who buy weapons and more importantly, restrict the sale of automatic weapons which are inevitably used in the frequent mass shootings.

Despite these suggestions finding favor with almost 90% of Americans including gun owners, nothing gets done as the wealthy *National Rifle Association* (NRA) has so many politicians in their pocket.

In other words, it is political corruption that lobbyists in the US sometimes facilitate.

Democratic hopeful Elizabeth Warren, has suggested that the system be abolished but it needn't be as lobbying works well in some countries.

In Canada and many European Union countries, powerful, rich corporations employ lobbyists but they cannot take advantage of the majority by bribing politicians.

Under their system, they do not allow the politicians to receive money. Instead, the lobbying is done transparently, through regulating agencies, under strict rules.

Consumers therefore are by no means as exploited as they are in the USA.

Other Democratic hopefuls who do not wish to go
as far as Warren, need to make their views on this
very important topic known.

For, can it be equitable for rich corporations both
local and overseas, to be able to bribe politicians or
even own some outrightly?

No, but the system does not have to be abolished,
only improved to serve the interest of the majority,
not politicians and their owners.

TAXATION AND SOCIAL SERVICES

One means by which American governments can help their citizens become happier, is, like Canada, increasing critical social programs.

Suggestions for programs such as: *free college education in public institutions and forgiveness of student loans* for lower income persons; *child care* for needy families; *reasonably priced health care* for those who have none; *maternity leave with pay* for working mothers etc., have all been put forward in the Democratic debates.

Can you believe that the super-rich USA is one of only two countries *in the world* that has *not* legislated maternity leave with pay for pregnant mothers?

Republicans love to bring up the topic of money whenever social programs to improve the welfare of its citizens are brought up. But they had no such concern when passing legislation to give billions of dollars in tax breaks to rich corporations.

Anyway, social programs to help Americans in their pursuit of happiness, can be financed through equitable measures such as;

a *Value Added Tax* (VAT), *wealth tax, increasing the percentage of income tax* on persons earning over a certain amount per year, *increasing/imposing inheritance and capital gains taxes.*

Again, it was Elizabeth Warren, who suggested a wealth tax, but there is nothing socialist about that, for even Switzerland, an *unapologetic capitalist country*, has such a tax.

Further, in a BBC report of Monday 24th June 2019, under the headline ***"US billionaires' group calls for wealth tax,"*** several American billionaires were reported as supporting such an idea.

The report begins; "Some of America's richest people are urging US presidential candidates to back a wealth tax on the super-rich to improve inequality and climate change.

America has a moral, ethical and economic responsibility to tax our wealth more," they said in a letter.

Signatories include investor George Soros, Facebook's co-founder Chris Hughes, and Molly Munger, daughter of billionaire Charlie Munger.

The group said they were non-partisan and not endorsing any candidate. A wealth tax could help address the climate crisis, improve the economy, improve health outcomes, fairly create opportunity, and strengthen our democratic freedoms. Instituting a wealth tax is in the interest of our republic. "

It continued;

"Among the 18 were a descendant of Walt Disney and the owners of the Hyatt hotel chain. Many in the group have been associated with progressive initiatives on issues such as climate change and the growing wealth gap.

The letter pointed out that fellow billionaire Warren Buffett has said *he is taxed at a lower rate than his secretary.*"

How much more inequitable can a system get than when you have a **wage earner** being taxed at a higher rate than the second richest man in the world?

The Brookings Institute has excellent analysis on the issue, as outlined in their article of March 14, 2019 entitled "*Americans want the wealthy and corporations to pay more taxes, but are all elected official listening?*"

Every registered voter should read that article.

Specifically, on wealth tax, they reveal that 61% of voters favor this.

Even Lloyd Blankfein, senior chairman of the wealthy and influential Goldman Sachs group, has come on board. For in a recent interview with Poppy Harlow on CNN, while admitting that he does not want to pay more taxes, he expressed a willingness to pay up *"if it can make the world less polarized."*

And it must, for *nothing is more polarizing than injustice.* And the unfairness of allowing the super-rich to contribute far less than they should, *is rank injustice.*

What makes polarization extremely dangerous too, is that it leaves the door wide open for despots of every political stripe, to exploit.

Listening to various discussions on the topic, I get the distinct impression that the only people who are really opposed to taxing the rich more and giving the middle class a break, *are Republicans lawmakers.*

Further, to finance critical social programs, it is not only that new taxes should be explored, but greater equity should exist, in how many existing taxes are calculated.

For example, an important driver of inequality the experts say, is the low taxes being charged on *estate tax*.

According to some, the only question should be, how much higher a percentage should those beneficiaries be required to pay.

Rational experts also say that *capital gains tax* should *not* be taxed at a lower rate than tax on income.

But it is, for capital gains has a top rate of 20 percent, whereas the top rate for salaries and wages is 37 percent.

So, while the US GDP is growing beautifully, real wages for the majority are barely increasing after being adjusted for inflation, while the gap between the rich and poor grows even wider.

Isn't it horrendous that in a wealthy country like the USA, 40% of adults cannot cover a $400 emergency expense? (Source CNN money).

As an outsider, it appears to me that the choices that American voters have in front of them for 2020, are quite good.

For a few of the Democratic hopefuls have been putting forward workable ideas that can help ordinary citizens become successful *in the pursuit of happiness,* something which has been very elusive for the majority so far.

However, even if Trump is impeached and banned from ever running again, because the GOP has become so sick, they have nothing to offer independent minded people.

For this is the 21st century, so *Jim Crow* must never ride again.

As to the socialists, they are shouting in the wind for the vibrant market economy in the USA can never fall under the control of bureaucrats and failed politicians.